Beheaded

The book of revelation made simple with commentary.

Dina M. Jones

Beheaded by Dina M. Jones.

©2017 Dina M. Jones. All rights reserved.

No part of this book may be reproduced in any written, electronic, recording, or photocopying without written permission of the publisher or author. The exception would be in the case of brief quotations embodied in the critical articles or reviews and pages where permission is specifically granted by the publisher or author.

Although every precaution has been taken to verify the accuracy of the information contained herein, the author and publisher assume no responsibility for any errors or omissions.

To my mother,
Shirley C. Jones,
I love you and thank you,
For placing me on the road to Doomsday.

Contents

Introduction vii
Foreword ix
Chapter 1 1
Chapter 2 9
Chapter 3 23
Chapter 4 33
Chapter 5 37
Chapter 6 41
Chapter 7 53
Chapter 8 59
Chapter 9 63
Chapter 10 69
Chapter 11 75
Chapter 12 81
Chapter 13A 91
Chapter 13B 101
Chapter 14 107
Chapter 15 113
Chapter 16 117
Chapter 17 125
Chapter 18 133
Chapter 19 157
Chapter 20 165
Chapter 21 171
Chapter 22 179
Acknowledgements 185
Bibliography 187

Introduction

This is the book of revelation from the Bible in its entirety with my explanation of each passage along with commentary. It is explained simply so that a nonbeliever in Christ, a believer in Christ, ANYONE, can understand it.

For many years, I have studied this book and didn't understand some of it. I wanted to understand ALL OF IT.

Finally, I found someone who could explain it to me and it was a blessing. I wanted to give the world this blessing by returning the favor. This book is written in truth and with humor.

Paragraphs in italics are the words spoken by Jesus. There are some exceptions. Paragraphs starting with numbers are the actual bible verses from the KJV bible.

If you are having trouble reading the Bible verses especially if you are new to the Bible and Revelation, just read my interpretation, it is less complicated and scary until you become comfortable.

Foreword

Doomsday. That's the word my mother used ever since I was a little girl. She said it for many scenarios, such as, "Don't have me waiting until doomsday!" "That will take until doomsday!" And many other applications of the word "doomsday."

One day, having heard that word a gazillion times, I asked my mom, "What is Doomsday?" My mother, not one to mince her words or sugarcoat anything, even for a very young child replied, "Oh, it's the day when the world will end." Wait? Say what now? I just got here! What in the heck is going on with this place? And so the journey began. I had to find out more about this world ending and what the heck do I do about that! But more on that in the future.

You are reading this book right now. It is much more important than my Christian life story, thoughts, hopes, and dreams. It is for every person alive right now on this earth. It is THE most important book you will ever read in your life. FOR your life. It is the book of revelation. Explained in simple terms, so that ANYONE can understand it. It is meant to be understood for the world in which we are living now.

Simply stated, I wanted to tell the truth. I wanted to be a real person with flaws, hopes, dreams, shortcomings, heartache, and also fear, not some "holier than thou" type of preaching individual who can do no wrong. I am just a human. I am not perfect. And I'm not your average Christian. For the Bible states, there is NONE righteous, no, not one. No one on this earth has the right to make another individual feel less than or ashamed, based on faith. The Bible states that we need to remove the plank from our OWN eye BEFORE we try to remove the splinter from someone else's eye! In other words, God is saying, you have your own flawed crap to deal with, quit trying to fix OTHER people's crap. Mind your own business!

We ALL fall short of the glory of God. We are all equal with the same opportunity to go to heaven as anyone that has ever lived or is alive on this earth! I wanted, with the writing of this book, to do my part, to let God use me as a means of conveying His message of the gospel, the opportunity of everlasting life to every living soul upon this earth.

Jesus came to heal the sick. Not just physically sick, but spiritually sick. Does a healthy person need to call 911? No. Only those in need of immediate attention of losing their lives. Although that is a metaphor, in actuality, it's the truth. A great number of mankind is in danger of losing their "life." Their REAL LIFE. Their souls. For all eternity. Call 911. Now. Call on the name of Jesus Christ as your lord and savior. Believe that He died for you and is alive today, seated at the right hand of the Father. He loves you and wants all of mankind to see the kingdom of God that no flesh should perish.

To those who are believers in Jesus, you need to call 911 as well. Although your soul does not need immediate attention, your knowledge of the events God has planned IS an emergency! The book of revelation was written just for that purpose! The Bible speaks about Jesus coming as a thief in the night. Basically, that is for the unbelievers of this world who reject Christ. But it also applies to believers who don't know what to expect from future events because you haven't learned what is in the book of revelation. I wrote it as plainly as I could through studying (YEARS worth!) prayer and discernment. "Call 911" by reading this book. Now. May God bless you all. Amen.

Chapter 1

1 The Revelation of Jesus Christ, which God gave unto him, to shew unto his servants things which must shortly come to pass; and he sent and signified *it* by his angel unto his servant John:

An angel gave this revelation from God the father regarding the various roles of Jesus Christ in future events, to a believer named John. This is to show believers things that will happen in our world very soon. Note: This is not the same John from the book of John. Occasionally, he is referred to as John of Patmos.

2 Who bare record of the word of God, and of the testimony of Jesus Christ, and of all things that he saw.

John recorded his observations and the things he heard regarding the word of God and Jesus Christ.

3 Blessed *is* he that readeth, and they that hear the words of this prophecy, and keep those things which are written therein: for the time *is* at hand.

Everyone alive on this earth that reads, hears, and remembers the book of revelation is blessed. All believers want a blessing from God. This is one of the reasons I wrote this book. I want everyone seeking a deeper understanding of God through the book of revelation to be blessed by understanding the words written in this book. Additionally, this verse warns us about the end of this world, as we know it is drawing closer every day.

4 John to the seven churches which are in Asia: Grace *be* unto you, and peace, from him which is, and which was, and which is to come; and from the seven Spirits which are before his throne;

John is instructed to reach out to seven, physical churches (not church ages as some believe) giving grace from Jesus Christ and the seven spirits of Jesus, which are before the throne of God. These seven spirits are mentioned in Isaiah Chapter 11 verses 1-2,

And there shall come forth a rod out of the stem of Jesse, and a Branch shall grow out of his roots:
And the spirit of the LORD shall rest upon him, the spirit of wisdom and understanding, the spirit of counsel and might, the spirit of knowledge and of the fear of the LORD;

Simply stated, these seven spirits are:

1. The spirit of the Lord.
2. The spirit of wisdom
3. The spirit of understanding
4. The spirit of counsel
5. The spirit of might
6. The spirit of knowledge
7. The spirit of the fear of the Lord.

5 And from Jesus Christ, *who is* the faithful witness, *and* the first begotten of the dead, and the prince of the kings of the earth. Unto him that loved us, and washed us from our sins in his own blood,

There is no one greater than Jesus Christ to speak as a witness to our humanity. Jesus lived as a human for 33 years. He was the first person raised from the dead into everlasting life. Yes, there were others who were raised from the dead, but those individuals died AGAIN. Jesus died once, rose from the dead, is alive and now sits at the right hand of God! He is greater than any king that has or will ever rule on this earth. Jesus loved us enough to die a painful death that allows us to wash our filthy sins in His clean, precious, Holy blood.

6 And hath made us kings and priests unto God and his Father; to him *be* glory and dominion for ever and ever. Amen.

When we believe in Jesus Christ, we become as important as kings and priests in the sight of God the father. Since Jesus has done that for us, He deserves all the glory and power over everything forever. The "amen" at the end of this verse signifies importance. It is very important that Jesus died to give us everlasting life and to escape the WRATH of God. Wrath is NOT tribulation (trouble). The difference between tribulation and the wrath of God will be referred to often throughout this book.

7 Behold, he cometh with clouds; and every eye shall see him, and they *also* which pierced him: and all kindreds of the earth shall wail because of him. Even so, Amen.

There is an "amen" at the end of this verse meaning it is significant. This is referring to the second coming of Jesus Christ. This is the other main theme of the book of revelation. The return of Jesus and His judgment upon unbelievers. Acts Chapter 1 verses 9-11 states,

And when he had spoken these things, while they beheld, he was taken up; and a cloud received him out of their sight.
And while they looked steadfastly toward heaven as he went up, behold, two men stood by them in white apparel;

Which also said, Ye men of Galilee, why stand ye gazing up into heaven? this same Jesus, which is taken up from you into heaven, shall so come in like manner as ye have seen him go into heaven.

When Jesus left the first time, He ascended up in a cloud. Everyone was watching. Two angels told everyone as they have seen the manner in which Jesus left, so by the same manner shall He return. This is important to grasp as it relates to other chapters as well as disputing the way Jesus shall return.

Additionally, the word "rapture" does not appear in the Bible. The Bible mentions believers being "caught up" in the clouds to meet Jesus. The unbelievers left here on earth will be the "kindred" wailing or crying. The 2nd coming of Christ starts God's wrath upon the earth.
My goal and my wish is that the knowledge gained from this book will help people escape that wrath.

8 *I am Alpha and Omega, the beginning and the ending,* saith the Lord, which is, and which was, and which is to come, the Almighty.

Jesus is the beginning and the end. This world was created by Him and it will end with Him. He is almighty!

9 I John, who also am your brother, and companion in tribulation, and in the kingdom and patience of Jesus Christ, was in the isle that is called Patmos, for the word of God, and for the testimony of Jesus Christ.

John is telling us that he is a believer. He is going through tribulation (trouble) because he was banished to the isle of Patmos for spreading the gospel of Jesus Christ.

10 I was in the Spirit on the Lord's day, and heard behind me a great voice, as of a trumpet,

John states he was in the spirit, spending time with God on the Sabbath when he heard a powerful voice. This voice was as powerful as a loud trumpet sound. Note: As a trumpet, not a trumpet. This is emphasized because there will be an actual trumpet sound upon Jesus' return to earth. This is NOT His second coming.

11 Saying, *I am Alpha and Omega, the first and the last:* and, *What thou seest, write in a book, and send it unto the seven churches which are in Asia; unto Ephesus, and unto Smyrna, and unto Pergamos, and unto Thyatira, and unto Sardis, and unto Philadelphia, and unto Laodicea.*

The voice says (Jesus is speaking) that He is the beginning and the end, first and last. Jesus tells John, what you see, write it in a book (the book of revelation) and send it to the seven churches (referred to in verse 4) located in:
Ephesus
Smyrna
Pergamos
Thyatira
Sardis
Philadelphia
Laodicea

12 And I turned to see the voice that spake with me. And being turned, I saw seven golden candlesticks;

John turned to see who was speaking to him. When he turned, he saw seven candlesticks made of gold. (What these represent will be revealed in the last verse).

13 And in the midst of the seven candlesticks *one* like unto the Son of man, clothed with a garment down to the foot, and girt about the paps with a golden girdle.

In the middle of the candlesticks, there was a man that looked like Jesus. (It was). He was wearing a long robe with a golden rope around His waist. Imagine meeting Jesus for the first time, you have HEARD what He may look like, but you are not sure. Initially, you would say He RESEMBLES the description of Jesus (the son of man) until you were certain of His identity.

14 His head and *his* hairs *were* white like wool, as white as snow; and his eyes *were* as a flame of fire;

John observed that His head AND His hairs were white like snow with the texture of wool. Wow. I can imagine someone having white hair but his head as well? That would be startling. John describes His eyes are as flames of fire. This description of Jesus is scary. It's not the description of Him as told in the gospels. This could explain why John said that this LOOKED like Jesus, but was uncertain. Yeah, I would be uncertain too!

15 And his feet like unto fine brass, as if they burned in a furnace; and his voice as the sound of many waters.

John describes His feet as resembling burned brass with a voice sounding like multiple sources of water. Envision the way the ocean sounds when it's violent and loud. This description is just as frightening as His other features.

16 And he had in his right hand seven stars: and out of his mouth went a sharp two-edged sword: and his countenance *was* as the sun shineth in his strength.

John witnesses Jesus holding seven stars in His right hand and a sharp sword coming out of His mouth. Jesus' face is as bright as the sun on a clear day. We are told at the end of this chapter what the seven stars represent.

17 And when I saw him, I fell at his feet as dead. And he laid his right hand upon me, saying unto me, *Fear not; I am the first and the last:*

When John saw all of this, he fell down. Yes, that would be my reaction to this description of Jesus! John states that Jesus touched him with His right hand and told him not to have fear. Jesus told him He is the first and the last.

***18** I am he that liveth, and was dead; and, behold, I am alive for evermore, Amen; and have the keys of hell and of death.*

Jesus states that He is the one who died on the cross, but is alive. He will be alive forever. Amen. Yes, amen! Jesus tells John He holds the keys to hell and death. Jesus was given those keys when He rose from the dead. Note: Jesus has those keys, not the devil nor anyone evil. This will be important in later chapters.

***19** Write the things which thou hast seen, and the things which are, and the things which shall be hereafter;*

Jesus tells John to write everything he has seen, all that is happening right at that moment, and future events that will be shown to John.

***20** The mystery of the seven stars which thou sawest in my right hand, and the seven golden candlesticks. The seven stars are the angels of the seven churches: and the seven candlesticks which thou sawest are the seven churches.*

Jesus explains what the seven stars were in His right hand and the seven candlesticks. The stars are seven angels belonging to the seven churches. The candlesticks are the seven churches. This is why it is incorrect to say the seven churches are different time periods or "ages." This is incorrect. The Bible states plainly these are seven actual buildings (churches) that once existed in what is now known as modern day Turkey. These seven churches were not far from the island of Patmos where John received the vision to write the book of revelation.

The book of revelation was written to seven churches instead of writing it once because there are specific messages for each church. Secondly, this served as a deterrent from fraudulent copies. If there are seven copies and one is different, it would be easy to find the fake one. Additionally, this was done to the entire bible. When confronted by individuals who dispute the validity and accuracy of the Bible we read today, the simple answer is, it's hard to fake many copies that are widely distributed.

All over the world, there are "textus receptus" which is Latin for "received text" of the Bible. All copies are compared against each other and found to contain the same writings. Yes, there have been fakes, but those are quickly disputed as being false when compared to other writings. Therefore, this provides proof that today's Bible is as accurate as when it was written.

Chapter 2

Unto the angel of the church of Ephesus write; These things saith he that holdeth the seven stars in his right hand, who walketh in the midst of the seven golden candlesticks;

Jesus is speaking to John telling him what to write down. Jesus is starting with the church at Ephesus.

2 *I know thy works, and thy labour, and thy patience, and how thou canst not bear them which are evil: and thou hast tried them which say they are apostles, and are not, and hast found them liars:*

Jesus tells this church He knows of the work, labor, and patience they possess. He knows this church cannot stand evil. He tells them they are good at revealing false prophets and doctrine.

3 *And hast borne, and hast patience, and for my name's sake hast laboured, and hast not fainted.*

Jesus refers to their patience again. He knows they have worked hard in the name of Christ by standing up for issues that are against His word. They have endured and continued to trust in God.

4 *Nevertheless I have somewhat against thee, because thou hast left thy first love.*

Jesus tells them He is somewhat mad at them because they have forgotten their first love, which is to preach the gospel and save souls.

5 *Remember therefore from whence thou art fallen, and repent, and do the first works; or else I will come unto thee quickly, and will remove thy candlestick out of his place, except thou repent.*

Jesus tells them, "don't forget where you came from, repent (ask to be forgiven) and return to preaching the gospel." Jesus warns them that if they don't, He will not hesitate to remove them out of their place in heaven. (Represented by the candlestick). He will come quickly to punish them.

6 *But this thou hast, that thou hatest the deeds of the Nicolaitans, which I also hate.*
Jesus states they have hatred for the misdeeds of another group of people, which He hates as well.

7 *He that hath an ear, let him hear what the Spirit saith unto the churches; To him that overcometh will I give to eat of the tree of life, which is in the midst of the paradise of God.*

Jesus says if you can hear, understand what is being said to these churches. Those individuals who "overcometh" they shall live forever in heaven. When the word "overcometh" is used, which it is used often in the book of revelation, it means whoever believes in God overcomes this world. Individuals who accept Him and the gospel into their heart shall triumph over all the hurt, pain and evil that exist. They will as well conquer this world! Thank you Jesus!

8 *And unto the angel of the church in Smyrna write; These things saith the first and the last, which was dead, and is alive;*

The next church Jesus addresses is the one in Smyrna.

9 *I know thy works, and tribulation, and poverty, (but thou art rich) and I know the blasphemy of them which say they are Jews, and are not, but are the synagogue of Satan.*

Jesus states that He knows their works, poverty, and the troubles they are experiencing at this time. Although they are literally poor, they are rich from doing good works. Jesus refers to those that SAY they are Jews, but are not. Jesus calls them the synagogue of Satan. That's harsh, but let me explain. The religion of Judaism does not acknowledge Jesus as the Christ in their beliefs or teachings. These individuals are mentioned in the book of Romans Chapter 2 verses 17-29, which states,

Behold, thou art called a Jew, and restest in the law, and makest thy boast of God,

This means the individuals that call themselves Jews believe only in the law (the Old Testament or Torah). The Bible states they puff themselves up or think they are better than everyone else because of their religious traditions.

And knowest *his* will, and approvest the things that are more excellent, being instructed out of the law;

This means they are aware of the will of God, but they won't follow His will. They know God's ways are better than their law (Mosaic law). That's part of the reasons Jesus came to earth, to fulfill the law, so we would have His way of living rather than the ways of men.

And art confident that thou thyself art a guide of the blind, a light of them which are in darkness,

This means these individuals are so confident that their way is the best religion; they feel "qualified" to tell and teach others who have no religion or belief system.

An instructor of the foolish, a teacher of babes, which hast the form of knowledge and of the truth in the law.

This means they teach the foolish unbelievers and those new to religion their knowledge and truth based only in the law (Mosaic law, Torah).

Thou therefore which teachest another, teachest thou not thyself? thou that preachest a man should not steal, dost thou steal?

This means that while they were teaching someone else, the Bible says, you should be teaching yourself. It says they preach that a man should not steal, but the Bible says they steal. The majority of synagogues charge fees/dues just to be allowed to sit in their seats! The gospel of Jesus Christ is free to all who will listen.

Thou that sayest a man should not commit adultery, dost thou commit adultery? thou that abhorrest idols, dost thou commit sacrilege?

This means God knows of those men who say they do not commit adultery (by worshipping idols) by claiming to hate idols, but have worshipped idols.

Thou that makest thy boast of the law, through breaking the law dishonourest thou God?

This means while they are boasting that they are better than everyone else by keeping the law, they are BREAKING the law of God by not believing His son is the Christ and that dishonors Him.

For the name of God is blasphemed among the Gentiles through you, as it is written.

This means there are people in this world who look at the religion of Judaism and it causes them to speak unfavorably towards God. Additionally, Christianity is known for blaming the Jews for killing Jesus.

For circumcision verily profiteth, if thou keep the law: but if thou be a breaker of the law, thy circumcision is made uncircumcision.

This means if you are circumcised and you obey the laws of God, including believing in Jesus as the Christ, you will "profit" from the blessings of God. If you break the laws of God, including denying His son as the Christ, being circumcised means nothing to God.

Therefore if the uncircumcision keep the righteousness of the law, shall not his uncircumcision be counted for circumcision?

This means whether a male is or isn't circumcised, he can be blessed by God. Judaism practices circumcision according to the law so that they can keep the covenant of Abraham and be blessed by God. Since Jesus fulfills the law, He says if you follow His ways and believe in Him, being uncircumcised does not matter to Him.

And shall not uncircumcision which is by nature, if it fulfill the law, judge thee, who by the letter and circumcision dost transgress the law?

This means males are born uncircumcised. If the uncircumcised males fulfill the laws of God by accepting Jesus, how dare you (followers of Judaism) judge those males, you who follow the (Mosaic) law to the letter but yet break the law (of God). Through their unbelief that Jesus is the Christ.

For he is not a Jew, which is one outwardly; neither *is that* circumcision which is outward in the flesh:

This means just because you are circumcised, which is a procedure that can be seen with the naked eye, does not make you a Jew.

But he *is* a Jew, which is one inwardly; and circumcision *is that* of the heart, in the spirit, *and* not in the letter; whose praise *is* not of men, but of God.

This verse means God considers EVERY man a "Jew," if he believes in Jesus Christ and keeps His laws in his heart. God states that a man's circumcision is in his heart and spirit. It cannot be seen with our eyes, but God can see it inside of a man. Moreover, these same men do not follow the law of the Torah and do not seek the praise of men receive the praise of God as a "Jew" in His eyes.

The Bible says those that deny Jesus as the Christ are against God or "antichrists". Not THE antichrist, just someone who is against Him.
1 John Chapter 2 verses 22-23 states,

Who is a liar but he that denieth that Jesus is the Christ? He is antichrist, that denieth the Father and the Son.
Whosoever denieth the Son, the same hath not the Father: *(but) he that acknowledgeth the Son hath the Father also.*

These verses state that you have to believe there is a Messiah and that the Messiah is Jesus. Unfortunately, Judaism teaches that Jesus was NOT the Messiah. Additionally, if you deny Jesus as the Messiah, you deny the Father as well. You have to accept the Father AND the son. Denying the Son automatically means you deny the Father.

Do not confuse race with religion. This is not against individuals who are of Jewish descent. God wants EVERYONE to believe in Jesus. This is expressed by Paul in his writings.

Romans Chapter 10 verses 1-4 states,

Brethren, my heart's desire and prayer to God for Israel is, that they might be saved.

This is to be our desire and our prayer that they will become believers in Jesus.

For I bear them record that they have a zeal of God, but not according to knowledge.

This means traditional Jews love God but not according to the truth, which is, Jesus is the Messiah.

For they being ignorant of God's righteousness, and going about to establish their own righteousness, have not submitted themselves unto the righteousness of God.

This means they are unaware of God's established truth (by following only the Torah and not acknowledging the New Testament) they are too busy creating their own truth. They are unwilling to believe on Jesus.

For Christ *is* the end of the law for righteousness to everyone that believeth.

This means Jesus Christ came to fulfill the law for everyone who believes in Him. In other words, you do not get to heaven by following traditions; you get to heaven by following Him.

Paul loved the Jews and earnestly wanted them to be saved. Christians should have the same attitude. Jesus told us to go into the whole world and preach the gospel to every kindred, nation, tongue, and people (that is the goal of my book). Jews, as a people, certainly fall into that broad category. Christians should seek to share the gospel with everyone (including them). Messianic Judaism aims to accomplish that task.

By the way, I am a follower of Messianic Judaism. Just by stating that can cause a follower of traditional Judaism to go ballistic! I have heard horror stories from our church members. Example: One of our church members was waiting in a doctor office. He began to talk with another patient. It was revealed that our church member is a Messianic Jew and the other guy followed traditional Judaism. The other guy said to our church member, "let's go outside so we can fight." Literally, fist fight! I was in total disbelief!

One reason for my disbelief was this guy wanted to fight (these are adult men). Secondly, I'm thinking, why does this guy want to fight over another man for telling him he is Jewish and believes Jesus is the Messiah? News flash: You CAN be Jewish AND believe in Jesus. If you don't believe, you should not fight someone who does believe! Crazy world. But I digress, back to the book of revelation.

10 Fear none of those things which thou shalt suffer: behold, the devil shall cast some of you into prison, that ye may be tried; and ye shall have tribulation ten days: be thou faithful unto death, and I will give thee a crown of life.

Jesus tells them, "do not be afraid of anything evil that comes your way." He tells them the devil is going to put some of them into prison to test their faith. This will last 10 days. He tells them to trust in God even if they die in the process and He promises they will live forever.

This verse is similar to the events that will take place when the antichrist is in charge. This is an advice to the Christians that are alive during that time. Some will be thrown into bondage or prison. The antichrist will start the beheadings (the title of this book) of Christians for not worshipping him or his image. Jesus is actually telling believers who are alive during this time, not to give up, even if you are beheaded, you will "overcome" and reign with Jesus forever!

11 He that hath an ear, let him hear what the Spirit saith unto the churches; He that overcometh shall not be hurt of the second death.

Everyone that can understand, hear what Jesus is saying to these churches. The believer that overcomes his troubles/persecution shall not be a part of the SECOND death. The second death is detailed in a later chapter. Let's just say for now, as a believer who is reading this book, you will be spared from the second death.

12 *And to the angel of the church in Pergamos write; These things saith he which hath the sharp sword with two edges;*

John is instructed to write to the church in Pergamos by Jesus. I like the fact that Jesus states something about Himself in the beginning of each letter. He says things like, "the one who holds the seven stars in His hand" or in this verse, He says, "He that has the sharp sword with two edges." It's a reminder as well as a threat! Jesus, in my opinion, is such a tough guy!!

I know those of you who are overly religious would disapprove of my using that term to describe Him, but He is. He makes statements that if He were a human man, He would be seen as a tough guy! Well, in my opinion, Jesus IS a tough guy who can back up everything He states and more. I came to realize this when Jesus states in John Chapter 10 verse 18,

No man taketh it from me, but I lay it down of myself. I have power to lay it down, and I have power to take it again. This commandment have I received of my Father.

I like the International Standard Version of this statement,

No one is taking it from me; I lay it down of my own free will. I have the authority to lay it down, and I have the authority to take it back again. This is what my Father has commanded me.

Simply stated, Jesus says no one can take His life unless He LETS them take it AND He can take it back! That is a bold statement to say in front of people trying to kill you. The coolest part about it is He can back it up! Those aren't just words. Think about it. Back to revelation.

13 I know thy works, and where thou dwellest, even where Satan's seat is: and thou holdest fast my name, and hast not denied my faith, even in those days wherein Antipas was my faithful martyr, who was slain among you, where Satan dwelleth.

Jesus tells this church He knows of their works, where they live and that Satan's throne is there. He tells them they have remained faithful to Him, even when their fellow believer Antipas died in the name of Jesus in front of them at the throne of Satan.

14 But I have a few things against thee, because thou hast there them that hold the doctrine of Balaam, who taught Balac to cast a stumbling block before the children of Israel, to eat things sacrificed unto idols, and to commit fornication.

Jesus tells them He is angry with them regarding a few things. They have preached a false doctrine. This caused the children of Israel to eat things sacrificed to idols, which is spiritual fornication.

15 So hast thou also them that hold the doctrine of the Nicolaitans, which thing I hate.

Jesus tells this church they have individuals there teaching false doctrine of another culture and He hates that.

16 Repent; or else I will come unto thee quickly, and will fight against them with the sword of my mouth.

Jesus tells them to repent (ask for forgiveness) or else His coming will be fast and He will use the sword from His mouth on them. In my opinion, that is some threat!

17 He that hath an ear, let him hear what the Spirit saith unto the churches; To him that overcometh will I give to eat of the hidden manna, and will give him a white stone, and in the stone a new name written, which no man knoweth saving he that receiveth it.

To anyone who can hear, understand what Jesus is telling this church. To him that overcometh, He will give Him new food to eat along with a white stone. Inside the stone is written that person's new name. No one knows these names except each person who receives one.

18 And unto the angel of the church in Thyatira write; These things saith the Son of God, who hath his eyes like unto a flame of fire, and his feet are like fine brass;

Jesus tells John to write to the church at Thyatira regarding His issues with them. We are reminded Jesus has eyes like flames of fire and feet that look like fine brass.

19 I know thy works, and charity, and service, and faith, and thy patience, and thy works; and the last to be more than the first.

Jesus tells this church He knows all of their service, faith, and patience. He knows they strive to improve themselves with every good deed.

20 Notwithstanding I have a few things against thee, because thou sufferest that woman Jezebel, which calleth herself a prophetess, to teach and to seduce my servants to commit fornication, and to eat things sacrificed unto idols.

Jesus tells them not to be mistaken, He is angry at them for letting a woman named Jezebel, who calls herself a prophetess, to teach as well as seduce believers into worshipping and eating things sacrificed to idols.

21 And I gave her space to repent of her fornication; and she repented not.

Jesus tells them He waited to see if she would repent (ask for forgiveness) of her idol worship, but she did not repent.

22 *Behold, I will cast her into a bed, and them that commit adultery with her into great tribulation, except they repent of their deeds.*

Jesus states that He is going to cast her into a bed (metaphorically) and every man that had sex with her (worshipped idols with her) will face tribulation (trouble/hard times) UNLESS each individual, admits their sin and repent. This is true for ALL sin.

23 *And I will kill her children with death; and all the churches shall know that I am he which searcheth the reins and hearts: and I will give unto every one of you according to your works.*

Jesus is going to kill her children (mankind) with death. Everyone will know Jesus can see inside of our hearts. He is looking for sincerity in our repentance. He will give the proper reward to each individual dependent upon what He saw in their heart.

24 *But unto you I say, and unto the rest in Thyatira, as many as have not this doctrine, and which have not known the depths of Satan, as they speak; I will put upon you none other burden.*

Jesus says He realizes some people do not have these writings. Some people do not know how far Satan will go to tempt them. Therefore, Jesus will not burden them with anything else.

25 *But that which ye have already hold fast till I come.*

Jesus tells them to keep believing in His gospel until He returns to earth. His second coming.

26And he that overcometh, and keepeth my works unto the end, to him will I give power over the nations:

This means the individual who does not give in to this world and remains faithful until He returns, will rule over nations. Jesus is speaking to every believer when He says we will rule a nation. No elections required. We will be appointed by Him.

27And he shall rule them with a rod of iron; as the vessels of a potter shall they be broken to shivers: even as I received of my Father.

Believers will rule their nations with a rod of iron (enforcing the laws of God) just like Jesus will rule over everything and everyone with a rod of iron. If we get out of line, He says He will break us into pieces like pottery! He received permission to do this from God the Father. Jesus is talking like a "tough guy" again, except He can and WILL back up every word!

28And I will give him the morning star.

Believers will be as important as Jesus, but not equal to Him. Jesus is known as the morning star. It should be obvious that we will never possess the power He has, but it will be nice to be in His group of peers.

29He that hath an ear, let him hear what the Spirit saith unto the churches.

Everyone that can hear, understand what Jesus is telling the churches. These are lessons and warnings not only for the churches, but for every believer living today that "hear" these writings.

Chapter 3

This chapter continues where chapter 2 ended, with John's letters to the churches.

And unto the angel of the church in Sardis write; These things saith he that hath the seven Spirits of God, and the seven stars; I know thy works, that thou hast a name that thou livest, and art dead.

Jesus tells the church at Sardis He knows this church has a great reputation, but they are not doing those things anymore.

2 *Be watchful, and strengthen the things which remain, that are ready to die: for I have not found thy works perfect before God.*

Jesus tells them to revive their good works and make them strong. The good things that remain in their church are about to die. Jesus is not pleased with some things they have done.

3 *Remember therefore how thou hast received and heard, and hold fast, and repent. If therefore thou shalt not watch, I will come on thee as a thief, and thou shalt not know what hour I will come upon thee.*

He tells them to remember how they have received, heard and held on to the gospel and repented. Jesus warns them if they do not pay attention to the events going on around them, He will surprise them when He returns. This is a very misinterpreted verse. Many individuals hear this verse and say no man know the day or the hour of His return, He will come upon you like a thief in the night.

That is why believers as well as mankind should read the book of revelation. Jesus is revealing to us to read and understand the world we are living in, to know how to interpret the signs of His return. He says it Himself, WATCH! If you DO NOT watch (read and understand) then His return will catch you off guard and surprise you.

4 *Thou hast a few names even in Sardis which have not defiled their garments; and they shall walk with me in white: for they are worthy.*

Jesus says there are few among this church, believers, who have earned the right to walk with Jesus and wear white.

5 *He that overcometh, the same shall be clothed in white raiment; and I will not blot out his name out of the book of life, but I will confess his name before my Father, and before his angels.*

He that overcomes (all believers) will be dressed in white clothing. Jesus will not blot his name out of the book of life, but will recognize that person as worthy to be in heaven. Notice Jesus says "blot his name out of the book of life." Psalm Chapter 69 verse 38 states,

Let them be blotted out of the book of the living, and not be written with the righteous.

It is customary, in some religions, when an individual becomes a believer and is baptized, they believe that person's name is added to the book of life. Well, as far as most scholars can tell, the Bible does not mention names being added, but throughout the Bible, it mentions individuals will have their names taken or blotted OUT of the book of life. Do you know what this means? It means we are ALL written in the book of life. The Bible mentions our names were there BEFORE He created earth. It is only when we choose, using our own free will to turn our backs on God and His son, that our names are blotted out. Ephesians Chapter 1 verses 4-14 states,

According as he hath chosen us in him before the foundation of the world, that we should be holy and without blame before him in love:

This means God selected each and every one of us before creating the earth. It states we SHOULD BE holy and without blame as believers with love in our hearts. I emphasized the word "should" because although we become believers in Jesus, we are still HUMAN beings living in a fallen world. Some people say that is no excuse, but the Bible states there is NONE righteous, no, not one. We all fall short of the glory of God.

Having predestinated us unto the adoption of children by Jesus Christ to himself, according to the good pleasure of his will,

This means we were PREDESTINED to be children of God through Jesus Christ and His will.

To the praise of the glory of his grace, wherein he hath made us accepted in the beloved.

This means we are to praise Jesus for His glorious gift of sacrifice, which allows us to one day, be accepted into heaven through Him.

In whom we have redemption through his blood, the forgiveness of sins, according to the riches of his grace;

This means through the blood of Jesus, we are saved from an eternity of torment. Those who remain in sin will be tormented. We are made rich by His grace.

Wherein he hath abounded toward us in all wisdom and prudence;

This means Jesus came to this earth with all wisdom and good judgment.

Having made known unto us the mystery of his will, according to his good pleasure which he hath purposed in himself:

This means Jesus reveals to us the "mystery" of His will when we become believers (And anyone reading this book!) The mystery is that He wants everyone to go to Heaven. He wants to fellowship and love us as we love our earthly children, but God does not FORCE us. He wants us to choose to be with Him, to love Him, of our own free will. Additionally, this mystery is the answer to the question, "what is the meaning of life."

That in the dispensation of the fullness of times he might gather together in one all things in Christ, both which are in heaven, and which are on earth; *even* in him:

This means a day will come when Jesus will gather all believers as well as every good thing from heaven and on earth.

In whom also we have obtained an inheritance, being predestinated according to the purpose of him who worketh all things after the counsel of his own will:

This means believing in Jesus gives us a heavenly inheritance. We have been predestinated according to God's will. It is mankind who uses his free will to give up our inheritance.

That we should be to the praise of his glory, who first trusted in Christ.

This means we should praise God since He was first to believe Jesus would do His will by being crucified for our sins.

In whom ye also *trusted*, after that ye heard the word of truth, the gospel of your salvation: in whom also after that ye believed, ye were sealed with that holy Spirit of promise,

This means believers trust that Jesus is the Christ. Believing the truth of the gospel, is how we become "saved" (from eternal torment, hell) which is through Jesus. When believers fully accept Jesus into their heart, we become sealed with the promise of everlasting life.

Which is the earnest of our inheritance until the redemption of the purchased possession, unto the praise of his glory.

This means we wait for the 2nd coming of Jesus to give us our inheritance of everlasting life, which was given to us BEFORE this earth was formed. We are to praise Him and all His glory! Hallelujah!

Continuing in the book of revelation.

6 *He that hath an ear, let him hear what the Spirit saith unto the churches.*

Everyone who can hear, understand what Jesus is saying to these churches.

7 *And to the angel of the church in Philadelphia write; These things saith he that is holy, he that is true, he that hath the key of David, he that openeth, and no man shutteth; and shutteth, and no man openeth;*

Jesus tells John that He has the key of David and if He opens a door, no man can shut it. If He shuts a door, no man can open it. This means no human can change the will of God. At times, this is a hard concept to accept. It's our free will that tries to open doors that are shut by God. This can lead to wasted time and pain.

8 *I know thy works: behold, I have set before thee an open door, and no man can shut it: for thou hast a little strength, and hast kept my word, and hast not denied my name.*

Jesus knows the works of this church; He has opened a door for them that no man can shut. He knows they are growing weary in their works and in their faith. Jesus praises them for keeping the word of God and for not denying He is the Christ.

9 *Behold, I will make them of the synagogue of Satan, which say they are Jews, and are not, but do lie; behold, I will make them to come and worship before thy feet, and to know that I have loved thee.*

Jesus mentions the synagogue of Satan and the individuals who say they are Jews, but Jesus says they are lying and are not Jews (this was discussed earlier). He will make them bow down before believers in Christ and let them know that He loves His followers.

10 *Because thou hast kept the word of my patience, I also will keep thee from the hour of temptation, which shall come upon all the world, to try them that dwell upon the earth.*

Jesus tells them because they have remained patient and kept His word, He will keep them from the hour of temptation. Jesus is speaking to believers who are alive today with this verse. The time will come when the antichrist will rule on this earth and force mankind to worship him and his image as well as take his mark upon their forehead or right hand. It will be an hour of temptation for believers because individuals who do not follow what the antichrist commands, will be executed, most likely be beheaded (there is the title of this book again). Although believers will be tempted to avoid death by accepting the antichrist, he that accepts death shall overcome and receive a crown of life.

By the way, Christians will be here on earth when the antichrist is in power. Not for his entire reign of terror, but for some of it. This is during the tribulation. When the wrath of God begins, believers are taken away by Jesus. This will be discussed further in later chapters.

11 Behold, I come quickly: hold that fast which thou hast, that no man take thy crown.

Jesus states He will come quickly. We are to hold on tight to our faith during this tribulation (not wrath) thus preventing any man from taking our crown of everlasting life. The alternative is eternal torment. I'm holding on for dear life, literally.

12 Him that overcometh will I make a pillar in the temple of my God, and he shall go no more out: and I will write upon him the name of my God, and the name of the city of my God, which is new Jerusalem, which cometh down out of heaven from my God: and I will write upon him my new name.

The believer that overcomes these events will be seen as a member of heaven worthy to be in the temple of God. Believers will no longer be tempted or troubled. Jesus will write the name of God, the name of the new Jerusalem (which is currently in heaven) and the new name of Jesus upon them.

13 He that hath an ear, let him hear what the Spirit saith unto the churches.

Everyone that can hear, understand what Jesus is saying to these churches.

14 And unto the angel of the church of the Laodiceans write; These things saith the Amen, the faithful and true witness, the beginning of the creation of God;

Jesus tells John to write to the church of Laodicea that He is the Amen, the faithful and true witness. He was there at the beginning of God's creation.

15 I know thy works, that thou art neither cold nor hot: I would thou wert cold or hot.

Jesus says He knows of their works, it's neither good nor bad. He wishes either they were dead and cold or they were zealous and on fire for His gospel.

16 *So then because thou art lukewarm, and neither cold nor hot, I will spue thee out of my mouth.*

Jesus tells them because they are robotic in their faith, they are lukewarm, so He spits them out of His mouth. Many churches today are not on fire for God. They are just going through ritualistic sermons and traditions, essentially these churches have become boring. Church members learn nothing new and many church members lose the fire of the gospel.

17 *Because thou sayest, I am rich, and increased with goods, and have need of nothing; and knowest not that thou art wretched, and miserable, and poor, and blind, and naked:*

Jesus says this church is full of pride. He says they believe they are rich and are in need of nothing. They are sitting on a pedestal, but Jesus tells them they are wretched, miserable, poor, blind, and naked. They do not have what they THINK they have because of their indifference to the gospel. There is Jesus again, not afraid to tell the truth.

18 *I counsel thee to buy of me gold tried in the fire, that thou mayest be rich; and white raiment, that thou mayest be clothed, and that the shame of thy nakedness do not appear; and anoint thine eyes with eye salve, that thou mayest see.*

Jesus advises this church (and modern day believers) to "buy" His gold (the gospel) that has been tried in the fire (His crucifixion and resurrection) that this church and we may become spiritually rich. We should be clothed in white robes (accepting Christ as our savior) so our unrighteousness/sin is not apparent. We should put ointment on our eyes (realize what He has done for us) so we may see clearly. Additionally, the last line means open our eyes to the revelation of the Bible, to the signs which are revealed to us, so we are not blind or asleep as we navigate through these troubled times.

19 *As many as I love, I rebuke and chasten: be zealous therefore, and repent.*

Jesus states He has many followers that He loves, and because He loves us, He will correct us when we are doing disapproving things before Him. He tells them and us to be very excited for Him, His gospel and to repent! Have you noticed how He is always telling us to repent? That's because He knows we are imperfect and will ALWAYS fall short of the glory of God, even if we are believers.

20 *Behold, I stand at the door, and knock: if any man hear my voice, and open the door, I will come in to him, and will sup with him, and he with me.*

This verse, in my opinion, has a double meaning. One is that Jesus stands at the door of our hearts, He will knock (urge us in our spirit to believe in Him) we open our hearts to Him, He comes into our hearts then we are entitled to sit at His table. Another meaning is that Jesus will knock on an actual door, He will come in the place where we are, physically sit down and eat with us. Jesus wants to be our savior AND like a family member.

21 *To him that overcometh will I grant to sit with me in my throne, even as I also overcame, and am set down with my Father in his throne.*

For all believers who overcome this world, we will earn the right to sit at His throne. Jesus overcame this world, hell, the devil and death. He is seated at the right hand of the Father's throne.

22 *He that hath an ear, let him hear what the Spirit saith unto the churches.*

Everyone that can hear, understand what Jesus is telling these churches.

Chapter 4

1 After this I looked, and, behold, a door *was* opened in heaven: and the first voice which I heard *was* as it were of a trumpet talking with me; which said, Come up hither, and I will shew thee things which must be hereafter.

After John wrote the seven letters, he saw a door open in heaven. There was a voice that was loud LIKE A TRUMPET, but not an actual trumpet. The voice instructed John to come up to heaven. He was shown future events.
Many people will point to this verse as proof that the "rapture" will happen BEFORE the tribulation. Jesus is talking to John, who is ONE man. One man is NOT a multitude of believers. John states that the voice SOUNDED like a trumpet, but it's not a trumpet. Remember the controversy with the trumpet sound is there will be a trumpet blast announcing Jesus coming out of the clouds to gather the elect (Believers). This verse is NOT about the rapture.

2 And immediately I was in the spirit: and, behold, a throne was set in heaven, and *one* sat on the throne.

John was in the spirit. The rapture involves changing our current body (for Christians that are alive when He returns) to a heavenly body. This is called translation. We shall be changed in the twinkling of an eye. John observed a throne in heaven and upon the throne was seated one entity.

3 And he that sat was to look upon like a jasper and a sardine stone: and *there was* a rainbow round about the throne, in sight like unto an emerald.

The entity was as beautiful as precious stones. There was a rainbow around the throne which glistened as an emerald.

4 And round about the throne *were* four and twenty seats: and upon the seats I saw four and twenty elders sitting, clothed in white raiment; and they had on their heads crowns of gold.

Surrounding the throne were 24 seats. Twenty-four elders (ministers/pastors) sat in the seats. They wore white clothing and crowns of gold upon their heads.

5 And out of the throne proceeded lightnings and thunderings and voices: and *there were* seven lamps of fire burning before the throne, which are the seven Spirits of God.

John heard thunder, lightning, and voices coming out of the throne. Sounds like a bad storm here on earth. There were seven lamps of fire burning before the throne. Remember the seven spirits of Jesus (God) mentioned in the beginning? These are the same seven spirits.

6 And before the throne *there was* a sea of glass like unto crystal: and in the midst of the throne, and round about the throne, *were* four beasts full of eyes before and behind.

John saw beautiful glass like crystal and as large as the sea. In the midst of all of this, standing around the throne, were four beasts that had many eyes in the front and back of their heads.

7 And the first beast *was* like a lion, and the second beast like a calf, and the third beast had a face as a man, and the fourth beast *was* like a flying eagle.

The first beast resembled a lion, the second, a calf, the third had a face like a man, and the fourth, like an eagle. This would be a scary sight to behold. These "beasts" have many eyes in the front AND back of their heads. This certainly is not anything we have ever seen!

8 And the four beasts had each of them six wings about *him*; and *they were* full of eyes within: and they rest not day and night, saying, Holy, holy, holy, Lord God Almighty, which was, and is, and is to come.

All four beasts had six wings. They did not rest day nor night. They praised the Lord continually. The Bible mentions these beings several times, calling them either living creatures or seraphim. Seraphim refers to the number six which are the number of wings each beast possess.

Additionally, the Bible speaks of "beasts" that have four wings each with four faces. They are called either living creatures or cherubim. Cherubim refers to their four wings. When I think of the word, cherubim, I think of cherubs. The cute, little red cheeked angel baby in a diaper with or without a bow and arrow. These "cherubs" have FOUR FACES! That's a horror movie, not anything romantic!

9 And when those beasts give glory and honour and thanks to him that sat on the throne, who liveth for ever and ever,

The beasts worship Jesus giving Him all the glory and honor.

10 The four and twenty elders fall down before him that sat on the throne, and worship him that liveth for ever and ever, and cast their crowns before the throne, saying,

While the beasts praise Jesus, the 24 elders fall down at His feet and worship Him. They remove the crowns from their heads and throw them at His feet. This demonstrates that He deserves all the praise.

11 Thou art worthy, O Lord, to receive glory and honour and power: for thou hast created all things, and for thy pleasure they are and were created.

The elders say to Jesus, you are worthy to receive glory and honor because He created all things and He delights in His creations. This is another way to convey "what is the meaning of life." Jesus created everything because He wanted fellowship. This reminds me of some couples who will stop at nothing to have a child especially if they are having trouble conceiving. They want a part of them to love and cherish. Someone that gives them companionship.

God is our Father and we are His children. Sometimes, we are bad children, but just like earthly parents, we love our children even when they are bad. We have to discipline them from time to time and so does our Heavenly Father. This is where our trials and tribulations arise especially for believers. Sometimes it is God disciplining us when we sin. He does it through the Holy Spirit. That "gut" feeling you have that something is wrong or just not right is God trying to tell you not to do it. We, as humans with free will, usually over-ride or ignore that feeling and do it anyway.

I saw a story, told by a girl, who was hitchhiking. She was picked up by a couple, so she felt safe. They stopped at a restroom. In the restroom, the girl said she heard her conscience say, climb out of the window, don't go back to the car. She was not a believer in Christ. She heard this voice 2-3 times. She did not listen. Upon returning to the car, the guy told her he was taking her as his personal sex slave. She ended up being held by this couple, living under their bed, in a box for years. She escaped and lived to tell the story, BUT that still, small voice, (the voice of discernment or Holy Ghost) that gut feeling, tried to warn her and spare her of the nightmare she endured. We all should listen to that voice.

Chapter 5

1 And I saw in the right hand of him that sat on the throne a book written within and on the backside, sealed with seven seals.

John saw God the Father with a book in His right hand. This book had seven seals. These seals are important because they initiate the tribulation and release the four horsemen. Some individuals call these the four horsemen of the apocalypse, but that is incorrect. These horsemen are upon the earth long before we get to any apocalyptic events.

2 And I saw a strong angel proclaiming with a loud voice, Who is worthy to open the book, and to loose the seals thereof?

John saw a strong angel asking in a loud voice who is worthy enough to open the book with the seven seals.

3 And no man in heaven, nor in earth, neither under the earth, was able to open the book, neither to look thereon.

John states that they could not find a man in heaven, on earth, or under the earth to open the book.

4 And I wept much, because no man was found worthy to open and to read the book, neither to look thereon.

John cried profusely because no man was found worthy enough to open, look upon, or read the book.

5 And one of the elders saith unto me, Weep not: behold, the Lion of the tribe of Juda, the Root of David, hath prevailed to open the book, and to loose the seven seals thereof.

One of the elders (pastors) told John not to cry because Jesus Christ can open the book for He is worthy. Hallelujah!

6 And I beheld, and, lo, in the midst of the throne and of the four beasts, and in the midst of the elders, stood a Lamb as it had been slain, having seven horns and seven eyes, which are the seven Spirits of God sent forth into all the earth.

John saw in the midst of the throne, the four beasts, and the elders a Lamb that had been killed. This Lamb had seven horns and seven eyes, which are the seven spirits of God sent here to earth (Jesus). Remember the seven spirits? Here they are again.

7 And he came and took the book out of the right hand of him that sat upon the throne.

Jesus came and removed the book out of the right hand of God the Father.

8 And when he had taken the book, the four beasts and four *and* twenty elders fell down before the Lamb, having every one of them harps, and golden vials full of odours, which are the prayers of saints.

When Jesus had taken the book, the beasts and the elders fell down before Him. All of them (including the beasts) had harps and golden vials of odors (like perfume) which are the prayers of Christians. It is beautiful our prayers are saved by God. Many times I have thought to myself, what is the point or is God too busy to hear my prayers? But no, it's just the opposite, the Bible says He saves every last one!

Don't be discouraged by thinking God couldn't possibly care about me, I'm just one of millions. Don't put God into that little box! He is all knowing and omnipotent! He knows the number of hairs on your head! He loves all of us. Believers AND unbelievers! Your Heavenly Father knows your needs before you ask Him, He just needs you to ask Him! When you do, it means so much to Him that He saves it in a golden vial! That's glorious!

9 And they sung a new song, saying, Thou art worthy to take the book, and to open the seals thereof: for thou wast slain, and hast redeemed us to God by thy blood out of every kindred, and tongue, and people, and nation;

Everyone sings a new song about how Jesus is worthy enough to open the book. He was crucified for us and by His precious Holy blood; all of mankind has an opportunity to go to Heaven. Thank you Jesus. Praise your Holy name!

10 And hast made us unto our God kings and priests: and we shall reign on the earth.

Through Jesus, we are people with great authority and will reign on earth with Him.

11 And I beheld, and I heard the voice of many angels round about the throne and the beasts and the elders: and the number of them was ten thousand times ten thousand, and thousands of thousands;

John saw and heard the voices of many angels surrounding the throne. The number John saw was approximately 100 million. Wow. Truly an incredible sight!

12 Saying with a loud voice, Worthy is the Lamb that was slain to receive power, and riches, and wisdom, and strength, and honour, and glory, and blessing.

Everyone present said with loud voices how worthy Jesus is because He was crucified. Jesus gained power, riches, wisdom, strength, honor, glory, and blessing. Note: There are seven attributes listed. Seven is the number of perfection. Praise God!

13 And every creature which is in heaven, and on the earth, and under the earth, and such as are in the sea, and all that are in them, heard I saying, Blessing, and honour, and glory, and power, *be* unto him that sitteth upon the throne, and unto the Lamb for ever and ever.

This verse states that every tongue ever created, no matter where they are, be it heaven, earth, or hell, human and animal, is confessing Jesus Christ is Lord forever. Hallelujah!

14 And the four beasts said, Amen. And the four *and* twenty elders fell down and worshipped him that liveth for ever and ever.

John saw the four beasts and twenty-four elders fall down and worship Jesus who lives forever and ever. Amen.

Chapter 6

This chapter one of the most talked about since it contains the four horsemen. When studying this chapter, it's helpful to compare it with other end time prophecy verses. These verses can be found in Matthew, Mark, and Luke (the Olivet discourse). The most widely known is from the book of Matthew. We will use verses from Matthew to cross reference with Revelation chapter 6.

1 And I saw when the Lamb opened one of the seals, and I heard, as it were the noise of thunder, one of the four beasts saying, Come and see.

John observes the Lamb open one of the seals. One of the beasts, in a voice loud as thunder, tells John to come and see.

2 And I saw, and behold a white horse: and he that sat on him had a bow; and a crown was given unto him: and he went forth conquering, and to conquer.

John saw a white horse with a rider that has a bow. This rider has a crown that was given to him. This rider went out to conquer the world. It is said this rider is the antichrist (this will become more apparent in later chapters of revelation). The antichrist likes to copy and twist things that are of God. Jesus will be riding a white horse at the battle of Armageddon. Of course, the antichrist would want one as well, even if it is metaphorical. The rider has a bow, which is symbolic of warfare, think Native American Indians.

If you think about it, an arrow is fast and essentially silent. It may or may not kill you, depending on where it strikes you. Isn't that a similar result from committing sin? Sin is usually fast (acting upon impulses instead of deep consideration). Silent (usually done in secret) and depending on the sin, it may or may not kill you! This rider goes out to conquer, in other words, seeking those he can get to commit sin. The rider has a crown, which is a sign of power and authority. The antichrist who is of the devil, gives him his seat and power to rule over the earth.

3 And when he had opened the second seal, I heard the second beast say, Come and see.

John heard the second beast say to him, "come and see".

4 And there went out another horse *that was* red: and *power* was given to him that sat thereon to take peace from the earth, and that they should kill one another: and there was given unto him a great sword.

John saw a red horse whose rider had the power to take peace from the earth and cause mankind to kill one another. This rider was given a great sword. Although this rider has power, he does not have a crown. Matthew Chapter 24 verses 6-7 states,

And ye shall hear of wars and rumours of wars: see that ye be not troubled: for all these things must come to pass, but the end is not yet.

Jesus is telling His disciples that during the end times, there will be talk of wars, but don't be afraid because this must happen before the end of the age.

For nation shall rise against nation, and kingdom against kingdom: and there shall be famines, and pestilences, and earthquakes, in divers places.

Jesus states, nations and kingdoms will be fighting. He says there will be famines, pestilences, and earthquakes all over the world.

5 And when he had opened the third seal, I heard the third beast say, Come and see. And I beheld, and lo a black horse; and he that sat on him had a pair of balances in his hand.

John saw the third seal opened. The third beast told John to observe. John saw a black horse whose rider had a pair of balances in his hand. Balances were common for measuring items especially during financial transactions.

6 And I heard a voice in the midst of the four beasts say, A measure of wheat for a penny, and three measures of barley for a penny; and *see* thou hurt not the oil and the wine.

John heard a voice over in the area of the four beasts talking about prices of food items, with oil and wine set aside as the most important. Those two items, especially the oil are big business. Almost everyone consumes some sort of alcoholic beverage all over the world. These items, in their own ways, can lead a person to kill. Oil generates the love of money and greed. Wine (alcoholic beverages) can cause individuals to become drunk and to kill in the spur of the moment. This meshes well with the first and second rider's "missions."

Additionally, this verse refers to day laborers working for a "penny" for a day's worth of work. Putting that into today's prices, an unskilled laborer makes approximately $50-$100 for one day of work. Can you imagine paying that much for wheat and barley? Food prices are already outrageous! They are getting worse every day and that's just "regular" food. If it's organic or in short supply, you are going to pay higher prices. There is a corresponding parable that refers to day laborers receiving a penny for their work in the book of Matthew. The parable is all metaphorical. Matthew Chapter 20 verses 1-16 states,

For the kingdom of heaven is like unto a man that is an householder, which went out early in the morning to hire labourers into his vineyard.

The rules of getting into heaven, is like being a landowner. The landowner went out early to hire day workers. The landowner is God looking for believers.

And when he had agreed with the labourers for a penny a day, he sent them into his vineyard.

He found workers willing to work for a "penny" so he brought them onto his land to work. Through the gospel, God finds individuals willing to accept Christ as their savior. Our reward is not on this earth, it is in heaven.

And he went out about the third hour, and saw others standing idle in the marketplace,

The landowner continued to look for workers throughout the day. God continues to search for anyone willing to accept Christ.

And said unto them; Go ye also into the vineyard, and whatsoever is right I will give you. And they went their way.

When the landowner found more, he brought them onto his land to work. God sends His believers into His "vineyard" to work (spread the gospel).

Again he went out about the sixth and ninth hour, and did likewise.

The landowner continued his search for workers. God is continually seeking those individuals who will believe in Jesus.

And about the eleventh hour he went out, and found others standing idle, and saith unto them, Why stand ye here all the day idle?

It is close to the end of the day. The landowner found the last of the workers were not working, so he asks them, "why are you standing around not working?" As the end of the age approaches, God is asking the non-believers, "why haven't you accepted Christ as your savior?"

They say unto him, Because no man hath hired us. He saith unto them, Go ye also into the vineyard; and whatsoever is right, that shall ye receive.

The workers told the landowner no one has hired them, so he hired them and told them whatever work they do, they will be paid for it despite being late in the day. Some unbelievers say they have not heard the gospel or they do not understand it (Another reason why I wrote this book). God puts people and circumstances into their lives (like reading this book) to become believers, then He tells them to spread the gospel. Their reward will be in heaven.

So when even was come, the lord of the vineyard saith unto his steward, Call the labourers, and give them their hire, beginning from the last unto the first.

When quitting time came, the landowner told the foreman to gather the workers, give them their money, starting with the last to arrive. When God brings about the end of this age, He will have Jesus gather the "workers" (believers) and give us our reward.

And when they came that were hired about the eleventh hour, they received every man a penny.

The workers, who arrived at the end of the day, received their pay. God will send every believer to heaven, even if they accept Jesus on the day He comes back.

But when the first came, they supposed that they should have received more; and they likewise received every man a penny.

The early workers, who had been there all day, felt they should receive more money, but were paid a penny just like the later workers. Some Christians think they deserve extra rewards because they have been believing for years. I felt this way once upon a time. Not anymore. The reward, for EVERYONE, is not going to hell! That is payment enough! No more, no less! Praise God!

And when they had received it, they murmured against the goodman of the house,

The workers who had worked all day and only received a penny complained about the landowner. When troubles enter a long time believer's life, sometimes, they think, why is God letting them experience hard times. They feel they are special and do not deserve it. I know because I'm guilty of this as well.

Saying, These last have wrought but one hour, and thou hast made them equal unto us, which have borne the burden and heat of the day.

The workers who had been there all day complained saying, "those workers just got here and they are getting equal pay. We have been here all day working in the heat." Some individuals have been Christians for a long time carrying heavy burdens and feeling the "heat" of temptation. Some do not think it's fair to be equal with new Christians. They feel the new ones have not suffered as they have suffered.

But he answered one of them, and said, Friend, I do thee no wrong: didst not thou agree with me for a penny?

The landowner answered them by saying he didn't do anything wrong. He asked them if they had agreed to work for a penny. They did. God doesn't force anyone to become a follower of Christ. When you accept Jesus as your personal savior, you agree to His "terms and conditions" which is to live as morally righteous as you humanly can and tell others about the gospel.

Take that thine is, and go thy way: I will give unto this last, even as unto thee.

The landowner tells them to take their payment and go away. He says he is paying everyone the same amount. When long time believers complain to God about their troubles, expecting special treatment, I think this is EXACTLY what He would say to them!

Is it not lawful for me to do what I will with mine own? Is thine eye evil, because I am good?

The landowner says to them, "it is not a crime to do what I want with my stuff." He asks, "are you looking at me with hate just because I'm doing something good?" God can do whatever He wants because it all belongs to Him. We are not to harbor evil thoughts towards Him just because He wants to be fair to EVERYONE!

So the last shall be first, and the first last: for many be called, but few chosen.

The last line "for many be called, but few chosen," God has many believers in Jesus Christ all over the world and we are to spread the gospel in our own way, but some Christians are made to stand out. Think of your favorite television preacher, you wouldn't know them if they didn't stand out (chosen for that task). I feel this applies to my situation. I have been a believer for years. I was content with being "just a believer" but one day God "chose" me to write this book.

Let me restate what you have just read. This parable teaches that it doesn't matter to God when He calls you as a believer. Unfortunately, some Christians who have been believers for a long time think they are better than newer Christians. In the parable, the workers who had been working all day felt they should be paid more and found it an insult to receive the same amount of money as the workers who were there for only an hour. The landowner (metaphor for God) told them, you agreed to work for a penny and this man agreed to work for a penny. You were paid what you agreed to no matter how long you have been here. Plus, this is my land and I make the rules.

When we agree to become believers in Christ we are all the same in His eyes, whether it was 60 years ago or today! We all receive the same reward, salvation! Hallelujah!

Back to revelation.

7 And when he had opened the fourth seal, I heard the voice of the fourth beast say, Come and see.

John watched as the fourth seal opened. The fourth beast said, come and observe.

8 And I looked, and behold a pale horse: and his name that sat on him was Death, and Hell followed with him. And power was given unto them over the fourth part of the earth, to kill with sword, and with hunger, and with death, and with the beasts of the earth.

John saw a pale horse. The name of the rider was Death. Hell followed this rider. Power was given to him over the fourth part of the earth to kill with sword, hunger, death, and with beasts of the earth. Remember what Jesus said in Matthew Chapter 24 verse 7? Read it again. It states,

For nation shall rise against nation, and kingdom against kingdom: and there shall be famines, and pestilences, and earthquakes, in diverse places.

There are diseases that are caused from not having enough food to eat. You can die from hunger. Clearly, we can see the four horsemen are working together to bring about chaos or tribulation on earth. Their job is to lead us into sin and if we die in our sins, not believing or accepting Jesus as our savior, you are going to hell. That's why death and hell are together.

9 And when he had opened the fifth seal, I saw under the altar the souls of them that were slain for the word of God, and for the testimony which they held:

When Jesus opened the fifth seal, John saw the souls that were martyrs for the gospel and their testimony (believing and confessing that Jesus is Lord and savior.)
Matthew Chapter 24 verse 9 states,

Then shall they deliver you up to be afflicted, and shall kill you: and ye shall be hated of all nations for my name's sake.

10 And they cried with a loud voice, saying, How long, O Lord, holy and true, dost thou not judge and avenge our blood on them that dwell on the earth?

The souls are crying out to God with loud voices asking Him why He isn't angry and for Him to bring wrath upon those that have killed them when they were on earth.

11 And white robes were given unto every one of them; and it was said unto them, that they should rest yet for a little season, until their fellow servants also and their brethren, that should be killed as they *were*, should be fulfilled.

The souls were given white robes. It was explained to them that they are to wait a little longer for other Christians to be martyred. Everything happens as it should in due time. Additionally, verses 10 and 11 are evidence that the opening of the seals is NOT the wrath of God (it is tribulation). Otherwise, the saints would not be crying out for vengeance.

12 And I beheld when he had opened the sixth seal, and, lo, there was a great earthquake; and the sun became black as sackcloth of hair, and the moon became as blood;

John saw Jesus open the sixth seal. When this seal was opened, there was an earthquake, the sun turned black, and the moon was red as blood. That's a very scary scenario. This event ends the tribulation. It is the beginning of God's wrath.

13 And the stars of heaven fell unto the earth, even as a fig tree casteth her untimely figs, when she is shaken of a mighty wind.

These "stars" are believed to be meteors or they could be angels since angels are referred to as stars in the book of revelation. Either way, the actual stars are in place in later chapters. Moreover, what we normally call "stars" are too big to fall to earth.

14 And the heaven departed as a scroll when it is rolled together; and every mountain and island were moved out of their places.

Heaven opens up as a scroll. God is shaking the earth so hard that mountains and islands are moved. That's some earthquake! It would be over for me right here! My terror would be so intense! The only thing that would calm my fear (if I'm alive when this happens) is knowing this is the return of Jesus and I'm out of here! Praise the Lord!

15 And the kings of the earth, and the great men, and the rich men, and the chief captains, and the mighty men, and every bondman, and every free man, hid themselves in the dens and in the rocks of the mountains;

It's showtime! Every person on earth who has thought highly of himself, was selfish, narcissistic, and didn't need God in His life is trying to hide himself from this wrath.

16 And said to the mountains and rocks, Fall on us, and hide us from the face of him that sitteth on the throne, and from the wrath of the Lamb:

These individuals are begging to be hidden from God and the wrath. The Bible says WRATH! This is the beginning of God's wrath carried out by Jesus!

17 For the great day of his wrath is come; and who shall be able to stand?

The Bible uses the word wrath again in this verse. The day of HIS WRATH is right at that moment and who will survive. This is better than any Hollywood movie, the only difference is, this will be real. No CGI effects needed!

Chapter 7

Chapter 7 is a continuation of God's wrath from Chapter 6.

1 And after these things I saw four angels standing on the four corners of the earth, holding the four winds of the earth, that the wind should not blow on the earth, nor on the sea, nor on any tree.

John observes four angels standing in the four directions of north, south, east and west. They are holding the wind away from the earth, the sea, and the trees.

2 And I saw another angel ascending from the east, having the seal of the living God: and he cried with a loud voice to the four angels, to whom it was given to hurt the earth and the sea,

John saw another angel coming from the east. This angel held the seal of God the Father (more about this seal shortly). God spoke with a loud voice to the angels who all have the power to damage the earth and sea.

3 Saying, Hurt not the earth, neither the sea, nor the trees, till we have sealed the servants of our God in their foreheads.

God tells them not to hurt the earth, the sea, or any tree UNTIL the servants of God have their protective seal in their foreheads (the antichrist stole this from God by requiring the mark of the beast to be placed onto the forehead of his followers).

4 And I heard the number of them which were sealed: *and there were* sealed an hundred *and* forty *and* four thousand of all the tribes of the children of Israel.

John heard how many servants were to be sealed. It was 144,000, which is 12,000 from the 12 tribes of Israel. This mark is a form of protection as seen in later chapters of revelation. The purpose of the 144,000 is to have individuals on earth continue to preach the gospel. The individuals who accepted Christ as their savior BEFORE His return are gone to heaven. Yet, God is still trying to save mankind from hell. He truly loves us.

The 144,000 need protection from God's wrath while they are spreading the gospel on earth. When I was younger, I wanted to be one of the 144,000, but upon learning the details of their mission, I have changed my mind!

5 Of the tribe of Juda *were* sealed twelve thousand. Of the tribe of Reuben *were* sealed twelve thousand. Of the tribe of Gad *were* sealed twelve thousand.

6 Of the tribe of Aser *were* sealed twelve thousand. Of the tribe of Nepthalim *were* sealed twelve thousand. Of the tribe of Manasses *were* sealed twelve thousand.

7 Of the tribe of Simeon *were* sealed twelve thousand. Of the tribe of Levi *were* sealed twelve thousand. Of the tribe of Issachar *were* sealed twelve thousand.

8 Of the tribe of Zabulon *were* sealed twelve thousand. Of the tribe of Joseph *were* sealed twelve thousand. Of the tribe of Benjamin *were* sealed twelve thousand.

All twelve tribes are named with 12,000 represented from each tribe.

9 After this I beheld, and, lo, a great multitude, which no man could number, of all nations, and kindreds, and people, and tongues, stood before the throne, and before the Lamb, clothed with white robes, and palms in their hands;

After the 144,000 receive their seal, John saw a crowd of people that was too large to count. These individuals were from all over the earth. These people stood in front of the throne, before Jesus, wearing white robes and holding palms.

10 And cried with a loud voice, saying, Salvation to our God which sitteth upon the throne, and unto the Lamb.

The multitude said with loud voices, salvation to God the Father who sits upon the throne and salvation to Jesus (the Lamb).

11 And all the angels stood round about the throne, and *about* the elders and the four beasts, and fell before the throne on their faces, and worshipped God,

John saw all the angels, the elders and the four beasts standing around the throne. They fell down and worshipped God.

12 Saying, Amen: Blessing, and glory, and wisdom, and thanksgiving, and honour, and power, and might, *be* unto our God for ever and ever. Amen.

These angels said amen (so be it), blessing, glory, wisdom, thanksgiving, honor, power, and might be given to God forever. Amen. Did you notice? Once again, there are seven attributes given to God. Always seven, the number of perfection, being complete, or finished.

13 And one of the elders answered, saying unto me, What are these which are arrayed in white robes? and whence came they?

One of the elders asked John about the multitude who were wearing white robes. He asked him where they came from.

14 And I said unto him, Sir, thou knowest. And he said to me, These are they which came out of great tribulation, and have washed their robes, and made them white in the blood of the Lamb.

John answered him and said, "you know where they came from." The elder did know and told John these are the souls of individuals who came out of GREAT TRIBULATION (not wrath). These individuals have washed their robes and made them white in the blood of the Lamb. This is a very poetic statement. We are so full of sin that we are like filthy rags, but when we become believers in Christ, He "washes" us with His Holy "clean," sinless, blood. We become worthy as Jesus himself to wear white robes.

15 Therefore are they before the throne of God, and serve him day and night in his temple: and he that sitteth on the throne shall dwell among them.

Those who made it to heaven and are standing in front of the throne shall serve Him day and night. God is there with them.

16 They shall hunger no more, neither thirst any more; neither shall the sun light on them, nor any heat.

These individuals will not be hungry or thirsty anymore. They will not have sunlight or heat on them. Personally, I love the way the sun feels on my skin, but I have faith that the love of Jesus will feel even better.

17 For the Lamb which is in the midst of the throne shall feed them, and shall lead them unto living fountains of waters: and God shall wipe away all tears from their eyes.

Jesus, who is there at the throne, shall feed them and give them His living water. God shall wipe away all of their tears. Ironically, that last line has always made me cry. It is very touching to think that God Himself will comfort us and that we won't cry (hurt) anymore. Praise God!

Chapter 8

1 And when he had opened the seventh seal, there was silence in heaven about the space of half an hour.

John saw the seventh and final seal opened. Heaven was quiet for half an hour. Very dramatic.

2 And I saw the seven angels which stood before God; and to them were given seven trumpets.

John saw seven angels standing before God. They were given seven trumpets. These are known as the seven trumpet judgments. In later chapters, there are seven vial judgments. Some people think the vials come after the trumpets, they do not. They happen at the same time. It was just the way the Bible was written. This will be examined further and proven as we continue in revelation.

3 And another angel came and stood at the altar, having a golden censer; and there was given unto him much incense, that he should offer *it* with the prayers of all saints upon the golden altar which was before the throne.

John witnessed another angel holding a golden censor. He had an abundance of incense that was to be burned along with the prayers of all saints (believers) upon the altar in front of the throne. Remember the prayers of believers are so precious to God the Father that He saves them. Just as a loving earthly Father would save precious items given to him from his children. This should have special meaning for us. Anytime we think praying is useless, we should be reminded God saves all of them. Thank you Father.

4 And the smoke of the incense, *which came* with the prayers of the saints, ascended up before God out of the angel's hand.

The smoke of the incense and prayers rose up to God as the angel held the censor.

5 And the angel took the censer, and filled it with fire of the altar, and cast *it* into the earth: and there were voices, and thunderings, and lightnings, and an earthquake.

The angel took the censer, filled it with fire and threw it upon the earth. John heard voices and thundering. He saw lightning and an earthquake on earth.

6 And the seven angels which had the seven trumpets prepared themselves to sound.

The seven angels were about to blow their trumpets, one at a time. Each one, when blown, brings a judgment or plague upon the non-believers on earth. Remember, this is after the multitude of believers are in heaven and it's AFTER the tribulation. The wrath of God is about to begin on earth!

7 The first angel sounded, and there followed hail and fire mingled with blood, and they were cast upon the earth: and the third part of trees was burnt up, and all green grass was burnt up.

The first angel blew his trumpet. Hail and fire mixed with blood fell upon the earth. A third of the trees and ALL the green grass was burned. Can you imagine the raging fires all over the world? I'm afraid and the wrath is just starting!

8 And the second angel sounded, and as it were a great mountain burning with fire was cast into the sea: and the third part of the sea became blood;

The second angel blew his trumpet. An object, as big as a mountain, on fire, was thrown into the sea. This caused a third of the sea to turn to blood. I am told some people cannot smell blood. Unfortunately, I'm an individual who can smell blood. It is unpleasant. If the fires aren't bad enough, the constant overwhelming stench of blood would be too much for me!

9 And the third part of the creatures which were in the sea, and had life, died; and the third part of the ships were destroyed.

A third part of the animals in the sea died as well as a third of the ships were destroyed. The blood AND dead animals? Just the thought of that smell turns my stomach.

10 And the third angel sounded, and there fell a great star from heaven, burning as it were a lamp, and it fell upon the third part of the rivers, and upon the fountains of waters;

The third angel blew his trumpet. A star (probably meteor) fell burning as a lamp, and fell upon the rivers AND fountains. God is making sure to include all of the water, no matter where it is located.

11 And the name of the star is called Wormwood: and the third part of the waters became wormwood; and many men died of the waters, because they were made bitter.

This star is called Wormwood. The star caused a third part of the water to become bitter. This killed many people. By the way, the name Chernobyl means wormwood in Russian. Many of us remember what happened there. If you don't, look it up. It's interesting.

12 And the fourth angel sounded, and the third part of the sun was smitten, and the third part of the moon, and the third part of the stars; so as the third part of them was darkened, and the day shone not for a third part of it, and the night likewise.

The fourth angel blew his trumpet. A third of the sun, moon, and stars were affected. The third part of them became darkened, causing these things not to be seen in the daytime nor nighttime.

13 And I beheld, and heard an angel flying through the midst of heaven, saying with a loud voice, Woe, woe, woe, to the inhabiters of the earth by reason of the other voices of the trumpet of the three angels, which are yet to sound!

John saw and heard an angel flying around heaven with a very loud voice woe, woe, woe to anyone still on earth! There are three angels who haven't blown their trumpets yet. In other words, he is saying, if you think that was bad, it's going to get even worse!

Chapter 9

1 And the fifth angel sounded, and I saw a star fall from heaven unto the earth: and to him was given the key of the bottomless pit.

The fifth angel blew his trumpet. John saw a "star" fall from heaven to earth. This star is an angel and he was given the key to the bottomless pit (hell). Jesus gave this key to the angel. This angel has a name, which will be revealed later.

2 And he opened the bottomless pit; and there arose a smoke out of the pit, as the smoke of a great furnace; and the sun and the air were darkened by reason of the smoke of the pit.

The angel opened the bottomless pit. There was a huge amount of smoke coming out, that it caused the sky and air to be darkened.

3 And there came out of the smoke locusts upon the earth: and unto them was given power, as the scorpions of the earth have power.

Out of the pit and the smoke, locusts (from hell) came upon the earth. These are not ordinary locusts. They have abilities like the scorpions we see on earth now. Due to the fact that I don't like bugs, this is the verse that scared me tremendously when I was younger. This prompted me to learn how to escape being stung by a locust from hell! It was simple: Be a believer. Thank you Jesus!

4 And it was commanded them that they should not hurt the grass of the earth, neither any green thing, neither any tree; but only those men which have not the seal of God in their foreheads.

These locusts were not to touch the grass, anything green, nor any tree (there probably isn't much of that left from the fires)! The locusts were commanded to harm people who do not have the seal of God in their foreheads. Now do you see why the 144,000 had to be sealed first before returning to earth? They had to be protected from these horrific plagues. I'm overjoyed that I am not a part of this group. Protection or not, I do not want to be there.

5 And to them it was given that they should not kill them, but that they should be tormented five months: and their torment *was* as the torment of a scorpion, when he striketh a man.

The locusts are commanded not to kill, but they can torment mankind for FIVE months by stinging them like a scorpion. Remember, it's dark too.

6 And in those days shall men seek death, and shall not find it; and shall desire to die, and death shall flee from them.

People will be in so much pain, they will try to die, but unable to do it. God will be in control of death. No suicides allowed.

7 And the shapes of the locusts *were* like unto horses prepared unto battle; and on their heads *were* as it were crowns like gold, and their faces *were* as the faces of men.

These locusts look like little horses prepared for battle. They have heads that appear to have crowns of gold on them and faces like men. This would be the scariest insect of all time for me!

8 And they had hair as the hair of women, and their teeth were as *the teeth* of lions.

The locusts have long hair and teeth like lions. God, in my opinion, is very creative when He wants to punish the wicked.

9 And they had breastplates, as it were breastplates of iron; and the sound of their wings *was* as the sound of chariots of many horses running to battle.

The locusts have an outer shell, tough like breastplates of iron. The noise of their wings sound like chariots with horses running into battle. Imagine: it's dark, smoky, there is a horrible stench, and there are these insects that are not easily killed because of their hard outer shell. My heart would just stop from fright, but the Bible says death shall flee from them. No escaping this nightmare.

10 And they had tails like unto scorpions, and there were stings in their tails: and their power *was* to hurt men five months.

Again, they have tails like scorpions and will use them on mankind for five months. I understood it the FIRST time.

11 And they had a king over them, *which is* the angel of the bottomless pit, whose name in the Hebrew tongue *is* Abbadon but in the Greek tongue hath *his* name Apollyon.

The locusts have a king. He is the angel with the key to the bottomless pit given to him by Jesus. The angel's name in Hebrew, is Abaddon, in Greek, it is Apollyon. Some people think that this is the devil. It is not. Jesus took the keys from the devil when He conquered death and hell. Why would Jesus give them back to him? This angel's name means destruction. He is used by God throughout the Bible for various tasks.

12 One woe is past; *and*, behold, there come two woes more hereafter.

There are two more plagues.

13 And the sixth angel sounded, and I heard a voice from the four horns of the golden altar which is before God,

The sixth angel blew his trumpet. John heard a voice from the four horns of the altar made of gold that stands before God.

14 Saying to the sixth angel which had the trumpet, Loose the four angels which are bound in the great river Euphrates.

The voice told the sixth angel that he was to release the four angels bound in the Euphrates River. These angels are believed to be the same angels from the book of Genesis guarding the tree of life. Genesis Chapter 3 verse 24 states,

So he drove out the man; and he placed at the east of the garden of Eden Cherubims, and a flaming sword which turned every way, to keep the way of the tree of life.

Although this verse does not say how many, we know there are four directions, north, south, east, and west, which equals four. It is said they are there right now, under the water, still guarding the tree. What a terrifying yet awesome sight! Not only would you find where the Garden of Eden once stood, you would find the tree of life and these cherubim with flaming swords. When I read this verse for the first time, I imagined seeing this human like creature standing there, under water, glaring at me as I would approach it. I'm sure they are not friendly.

15 And the four angels were loosed, which were prepared for an hour, and a day, and a month, and a year, for to slay the third part of men.

The four angels were set free. They have been down there since mankind was banned from the Garden of Eden. That's a LONG time! Their new job is to kill a third of mankind.

16 And the number of the army of the horsemen *were* two hundred thousand thousand: and I heard the number of them.

The four cherubim are not alone. They are leading an army of 200 million.

17 And thus I saw the horses in the vision, and them that sat on them, having breastplates of fire, and of jacinth, and brimstone: and the heads of the horses *were* as the heads of lions; and out of their mouths issued fire and smoke and brimstone.

John observes special horses for this army. They have riders with breastplates of fire, precious stones and brimstone. The heads of the horses look like lions. They can spit out of their mouths fire, smoke, and brimstone. Horses that look like lions. Creative and deadly.

18 By these three was the third part of men killed, by the fire, and by the smoke, and by the brimstone, which issued out of their mouths.

The army will kill a third of mankind by spewing these items from their mouths.

19 For their power is in their mouth, and in their tails: for their tails *were* like unto serpents, and had heads, and with them they do hurt.

In addition to their mouths, the horses have tails like a snake, which will bite mankind. God is ANGRY with the wicked.

20 And the rest of the men which were not killed by these plagues yet repented not of the works of their hands, that they should not worship devils, and idols of gold, and silver, and brass, and stone, and of wood: which neither can see, nor hear, nor walk:

Anyone who remains alive through these plagues, did not repent of their sin for worshipping idols. Personally, I would have begged for forgiveness (repented) a long time before this!

21 Neither repented they of their murders, nor of their sorceries, nor of their fornication, nor of their thefts.

Moreover, the wicked did not repent for their murders, sorcery, idol worship and stealing. Non-believers today call God an "imaginary sky friend." Some think Christians are stupid for believing there is a God, but at that moment, after those left on earth have seen, SOMEBODY is causing these horrible, painful things. The wicked are hearing the gospel from the 144,000 and the two witnesses (discussed later). It's not like they are totally clueless. That, in my opinion, is truly an evil-hearted individual.

Chapter 10

1 And I saw another mighty angel come down from heaven, clothed with a cloud: and a rainbow *was* upon his head, and his face *was* as it were the sun, and his feet as pillars of fire:

John saw an angel come down from heaven surrounded by a cloud. He had a rainbow on his head, his face was as bright as the sun and his feet were like fire.

2 And he had in his hand a little book open: and he set his right foot upon the sea, and *his* left *foot* on the earth,

This angel held a little book as he set his right foot on the sea and left foot on the earth.

3 And cried with a loud voice, as *when* a lion roareth: and when he had cried, seven thunders uttered their voices.

The angel said something (we do not know what) with a loud voice like a lion. When he did this, seven thunders said something in return.

4 And when the seven thunders had uttered their voices, I was about to write: and I heard a voice from heaven saying unto me, Seal up those things which the seven thunders uttered, and write them not.

John was going to write down what was said, but a voice from heaven told him not to write it. People say the book of revelation is a mystery. It is not. The words spoken by the angel and seven thunders IS A MYSTERY because God is hiding this information on purpose. One day, we shall learn this mystery.

5 And the angel which I saw stand upon the sea and upon the earth lifted up his hand to heaven,

John saw the angel standing on the earth and the sea lift his hand towards heaven.

6 And sware by him that liveth for ever and ever, who created heaven, and the things that therein are, and the earth, and the things that therein are, and the sea, and the things which are therein, that there should be time no longer:

John states this angel swore (pledged) to God there will be time no more. This does not mean there won't be a measurement of time. This is explained in the next verse.

7 But in the days of the voice of the seventh angel, when he shall begin to sound, the mystery of God should be finished, as he hath declared to his servants the prophets.

This verse means when the seventh angel blows his trumpet, the mystery of God will be finished. Throughout the Bible when prophecy was shown or told to the receiver, it was a "mystery" to them. An example is the book of Daniel; he did not understand his end time prophecy neither did the disciples of Jesus. In the book of Daniel Chapter 12 verses 4-10 states,

But thou, O Daniel, shut up the words, and seal the book, *even* to the time of the end: many shall run to and fro, and knowledge shall be increased.

Daniel is told to seal up his prophecy until our time. We are able to go anywhere in this world (to and fro). Knowledge is increasing exponentially daily. We find new discoveries of all kind practically every day. Daniel's prophecy is for those alive today.

Then I Daniel looked, and, behold, there stood other two, the one on this side of the bank of the river, and the other on that side of the bank of the river.

This angel is described like the angel John saw standing with one foot in the sea and the other one on earth.

And *one* said to the man clothed in linen, which *was* upon the waters of the river, How long *shall it be to* the end of these wonders?

Someone asked the angel how long shall it be until the wrath of God is completed.

And I heard the man clothed in linen, which *was* upon the waters of the river, when he held up his right hand and his left hand unto heaven, and sware by him that liveth for ever that *it shall be* for a time, times, and an half; and when he shall have accomplished to scatter the power of the holy people, all these *things* shall be finished.

The angel swore to God and said that after three and a half years of pouring out His wrath, God will be finished. This is a more definitive explanation than the angel who said there will be time no longer.

And I heard, but I understood not: then said I, O my Lord, what *shall be* the end of these *things*?

Daniel heard, but did not understand. That's because the prophecy was not for his moment in time, but it is for us now.

And he said, Go thy way, Daniel: for the words *are* closed up and sealed till the time of the end.

Daniel was told not to worry about it. The words spoken to him were closed and sealed until it's time for the world to end.

Many shall be purified, and made white, and tried; but the wicked shall do wickedly: and none of the wicked shall understand; but the wise shall understand.

At the end of time, there will be many people who will become believers, be martyred and tested for their faith. The wicked shall continue to do evil and will not understand nor want to know about the wrath that is coming. The wise will understand (if you are reading this book, you are wise).

Return to revelation.

8 And the voice which I heard from heaven spake unto me again, and said, Go *and* take the little book which is open in the hand of the angel which standeth upon the sea and upon the earth.

John heard the voice from heaven. The voice told him to take the little black book from the angel that is standing on the earth.

9 And I went unto the angel, and said unto him, Give me the little book. And he said unto me, Take *it*, and eat it up; and it shall make thy belly bitter, but it shall be in thy mouth sweet as honey.

John approached the angel and asked for the book. The angel told him to take it and eat it. He told John that it will make him sick to his stomach, but will be sweet as honey in his mouth. This is explained in the next verse.

10 And I took the little book out of the angel's hand, and ate it up; and it was in my mouth sweet as honey: and as soon as I had eaten it, my belly was bitter.

John took the book from the angel and ate it. It was truly sweet in his mouth, but his stomach became bitter and upset. The eating of the book is symbolic. John doesn't "eat" a book, but the word of God. Matthew Chapter 4 verse 4 states,

But he answered and said, *It is written, Man shall not live by bread alone, but by every word that proceedeth out of the mouth of God.*

The word of God sustains us. The Bible gives us strength during the storms of life. We should turn to the promises of God to help us through those times.

Additionally, John's belly was made bitter because there are issues we find unpleasant in the Bible. We become Christians, but we are still human. We are not perfect. Our flesh struggles with sin and we can give in to sin, even as a Christian. Sometimes when we sin, we have a sickening feeling in our stomach. That is because we know the right thing to do, what the Holy Spirit is urging us to do, but we use our free will and go against God. We are to seek Him for strength and peace.

11 And he said unto me, Thou must prophesy again before many peoples, and nations, and tongues, and kings.

John is to write these prophetic words down to be shared with all of mankind.

Chapter 11

1 And there was given me a reed like unto a rod: and the angel stood, saying, Rise, and measure the temple of God, and the altar, and them that worship therein.

John was told to measure the temple of God, its structure, and the people that are worshipping inside of the temple. This is referring to the third temple in Jerusalem that has not been rebuilt.

2 But the court which is without the temple leave out, and measure it not; for it is given unto the Gentiles: and the holy city shall they tread under foot forty *and* two months.

John is told not to measure the outer court; it belongs to the Gentiles (Non-Jew). John is told the holy city shall be trampled upon for 42 months or 3 and a half years. There is a corresponding verse in the book of Luke Chapter 21 verse 24 stating,

And they shall fall by the edge of the sword, and shall be led away captive into all nations: and Jerusalem shall be trodden down of the Gentiles, until the times of the Gentiles be fulfilled.

Christians will be held captive all over the world for a short time until the return of Christ. This is when many Christians shall be beheaded for their faith.

Back to revelation.

3 And I will give *power* unto my two witnesses, and they shall prophesy a thousand two hundred *and* threescore days, clothed in sackcloth.

There will be two witnesses preaching and telling prophesies like the 144,000. They will be on earth during the wrath of God for 1,260 days starting right after the second coming of Christ. Remember, all Christians have been taken to heaven. God is trying desperately to save mankind from hell by having the gospel preached to the non-believers.

4 These are the two olive trees, and the two candlesticks standing before the God of the earth.

This is a metaphor for the two witnesses.

5 And if any man will hurt them, fire proceedeth out of their mouth, and devoureth their enemies: and if any man will hurt them, he must in this manner be killed.

If anyone tries to hurt the witnesses or succeeds in hurting them, the witnesses can make fire come out of their mouths and kill their enemy. The enemy MUST die in this manner.

6 These have power to shut heaven, that it rain not in the days of their prophecy: and have power over waters to turn them to blood, and to smite the earth with all plagues, as often as they will.

The witnesses have the power to stop it from raining. They can turn water into blood (not that there would be much left since the wrath of God turned most of it to blood already)! I'm thinking bottled water and personal supplies.

7 And when they shall have finished their testimony, the beast that ascendeth out of the bottomless pit shall make war against them, and shall overcome them, and kill them.

When the witnesses have completed their mission, the antichrist will fight them and kill them.

8 And their dead bodies *shall lie* in the street of the great city, which spiritually is called Sodom and Egypt, where also our Lord was crucified.

The witnesses' dead bodies will be in the streets of the holy city (Jerusalem) where Jesus was crucified.

9 And they of the people and kindreds and tongues and nations shall see their dead bodies three days and an half, and shall not suffer their dead bodies to be put in graves.

The entire world (the internet?) will see them dead in the street for three and a half days. No one will bury them.

10 And they that dwell upon the earth shall rejoice over them, and make merry, and shall send gifts one to another; because these two prophets tormented them that dwelt on the earth.

Those left here on earth (and not killed during the plagues) shall be overjoyed they are dead since the witnesses tormented them. They will be so happy that they are going to send gifts to each other. Imagine that, receiving gifts because two prophets are dead. Happy dead prophets day, dear! Cruel.

11 And after three days and an half the Spirit of life from God entered into them, and they stood upon their feet; and great fear fell upon them which saw them.

After the allotted time has passed, God brings the witnesses back to life and they stand up. This frightens everyone who observes this event. I'm sure it would, since we haven't seen dead bodies come back to life after almost four days. Maybe when Jesus was on earth, but not this generation.

12 And they heard a great voice from heaven saying unto them, Come up hither. And they ascended up to heaven in a cloud; and their enemies beheld them.

A great voice from heaven called out to the witnesses to come up to heaven. They went to heaven in a cloud and all of their enemies watched as they left this earth. Can you imagine the look on everyone's face? Beyond stunned, I'm sure.

13 And the same hour was there a great earthquake, and the tenth part of the city fell, and in the earthquake were slain of men seven thousand: and the remnant were affrighted, and gave glory to the God of heaven.

Within the hour of their departure, there was a great earthquake. A tenth of the city fell and 7,000 men (possibly men, women and children) were killed. The Christians watching in heaven gave glory to God the Father.

14 The second woe is past; *and*, behold, the third woe cometh quickly.

There have been two woes. There is one left.

15 And the seventh angel sounded; and there were great voices in heaven, saying, The kingdoms of this world are become *the kingdoms* of our Lord, and of his Christ; and he shall reign for ever and ever.

The seventh angel blew his trumpet. Powerful voices were speaking in heaven. They said that the kingdoms of this world (on earth) have become the kingdoms of Jesus Christ. Jesus Christ shall reign for eternity. This is the verse that demonstrates the end of the wrath of God and is the beginning of the 1,000 year reign of Christ. Technically, this is the end of the book of revelation. In Chapter 12, the story begins again, but starts with the birth of Christ. Why tell two versions of the story? Well, there are four versions of the gospel in Matthew, Mark, Luke, and John. This half of revelation is told with additional detail of topics already covered. This is what causes the misconception of the vials coming after the trumpets. Yes, it may appear that way, but only if you do not realize the book of revelation has ended in Chapter 11.

16 And the four and twenty elders, which sat before God on their seats, fell upon their faces, and worshipped God,

The twenty-four elders fell down on their faces and worshipped God.

17 Saying, We give thee thanks, O Lord God Almighty, which art, and wast, and art to come; because thou hast taken to thee thy great power, and hast reigned.

They said to Jesus they give Him thanks, for He is Lord God Almighty, who is, who was, and is to come because He has taken for Himself great power and has reigned.

18 And the nations were angry, and thy wrath is come, and the time of the dead, that they should be judged, and that thou shouldest give reward unto thy servants the prophets, and to the saints, and them that fear thy name, small and great; and shouldest destroy them which destroy the earth.

Those upon the earth are angry because the wrath of God is being poured out upon them. Jesus will judge the dead and He will reward servants, the prophets, saints, and all who fear His name (these are all believers who have made it to heaven, but because of their distinction, will receive different rewards for their work (how they helped to spread the gospel). Jesus will destroy those who have destroyed the earth.

19 And the temple of God was opened in heaven, and there was seen in his temple the ark of his testament: and there were lightnings, and voices, and thunderings, and an earthquake, and great hail.

The temple of God was opened in heaven. Inside was the Ark of the Covenant. There was lightning and thunder. As this is happening in heaven, on earth, there is the biggest earthquake, bigger than any other and great hail. The end. This is the last woe? An earthquake and hail? Remember, the second version of revelation gives greater details. Let's begin, again.

Chapter 12

The beginning. This chapter is very metaphorical and very misinterpreted. I have studied this chapter extensively. Due to the metaphors, there are many references pulled from several chapters to explain the meaning of the verses. Having gained knowledge through prayer and discernment, I will share my interpretation of this chapter.

1 And there appeared a great wonder in heaven; a woman clothed with the sun, and the moon under her feet, and upon her head a crown of twelve stars:

The woman is the CITY of Jerusalem, just the city. As we go further along in this chapter, this will become obvious, it is not Israel (Israel is metaphorically male). Additionally, Ezekiel Chapter 5 verse 5 states,

Thus saith the Lord GOD; This *is* Jerusalem: I have set it in the midst of the nations and countries *that are* round about her.

Note how it states "her."

2 Kings Chapter 19 verse 21 uses female terms by stating,

This *is* the word that the LORD hath spoken concerning him; The virgin the daughter of Zion hath despised thee, *and* laughed thee to scorn; the daughter of Jerusalem hath shaken her head at thee.

Galatians Chapter 4 verse 26 states,

But Jerusalem which is above is free, which is the mother of us all.

Mother, not father. Just as other cities are metaphorically a woman such as the city of Babylon.

It states that she is clothed with the sun. According to the Jewish sages, (wise men whose writings were passed down through the ages) this is a metaphor for the nations of the world. Remember Ezekiel Chapter 5 verse 5 states,

Thus saith the Lord GOD; This *is* Jerusalem: I have set it in the midst of the nations and countries *that are* round about her.

The verse states "the moon under her feet." According to the Jewish sages, the moon represents Jewish people. Well, if the "moon" *are* under her feet, under Jerusalem, these are the dead who are buried in Jerusalem's earth. The crown of twelve stars are, of course, the 12 tribes.

2 And she being with child cried, travailing in birth, and pained to be delivered.

Jerusalem is about to give "birth" to Jesus Christ our Savior. Zechariah Chapter 9 verse 9 states,

Rejoice greatly, O daughter of Zion; shout, O daughter of Jerusalem: behold, thy King cometh unto thee: he *is* just, and having salvation; lowly, and riding upon an ass, and upon a colt the foal of an ass.

Again, note the female references to Jerusalem.

3 And there appeared another wonder in heaven; and behold a great red dragon, having seven heads and ten horns, and seven crowns upon his heads.

The dragon is the devil or Satan. The seven heads, ten horns and seven crowns will be discussed in other chapters.

4 And his tail drew the third part of the stars of heaven, and did cast them to the earth: and the dragon stood before the woman which was ready to be delivered, for to devour her child as soon as it was born.

The word, tail, in the Bible represents subjection (to bring under control) Satan managed to bring a third of the angels (now demons) under his control. They were thrown out of heaven, along with himself and was cast down to earth.

Remember the devil wanted to kill Jesus upon His birth using King Herod. King Herod instructed the three wise men to send word of Jesus birth to him and pretended he wanted to come worship Jesus. In reality, he wanted to kill Jesus. The wise men were wise (pun intended!) and realized his scheme. They did not send word to the king and returned home by another route.

King Herod became so angry that he ordered the death of all males under the age of two! Jesus avoided this slaughter because Joseph was warned by an angel to take Jesus to Egypt.

5 And she brought forth a man child, who was to rule all nations with a rod of iron: and her child was caught up unto God, and *to* his throne.

Jesus is born. Someday, He will return to earth and rule with a rod of iron. After His resurrection, He went to heaven where He currently sits at the right hand of God upon the throne.

6 And the woman fled into the wilderness, where she hath a place prepared of God, that they should feed her there a thousand two hundred *and* threescore days.

This verse is referring to the third temple being built in Jerusalem. Isaiah Chapter 64 verse 10 states,

Thy holy cities are a wilderness, Zion is a wilderness, Jerusalem a desolation.

Jerusalem will be safe, holy, and used as a place of worship as well as sacrifice for 1,260 days before the abomination of desolation. The abomination of desolation is when the antichrist goes into the third temple and declares himself God. There are three passages from the book of Daniel that mentions this event.

Daniel Chapter 9 verse 27 states,

And he shall confirm the covenant with many for one week: and in the midst of the week he shall cause the sacrifice and the oblation to cease, and for the overspreading of abominations he shall make *it* desolate, even until the consummation, and that determined shall be poured upon the desolate.

Theologians interpret this "week" as seven years. In the midst (middle) of the week, which is three and a half years, the antichrist stop the sacrifices and cause the abomination of desolation.

Daniel Chapter 11 verse 31 states,

And arms shall stand on his part, and they shall pollute the sanctuary of strength, and shall take away the daily *sacrifice*, and they shall place the abomination that maketh desolate.

Lastly, Daniel Chapter 12 verse 11 states,

And from the time *that* the daily *sacrifice* shall be taken away, and the abomination that maketh desolate set up, *there shall be* a thousand, two hundred and ninety days (1,290 days). Notice, there are 30 days from when the woman is safe (1,260 days) and when the sacrifices stop before the abomination of desolation. Possibly it will take thirty days of red tape to stop the daily sacrifices at the third temple, especially since the "treaty" was for seven years.

7 And there was war in heaven: Michael and his angels fought against the dragon; and the dragon fought and his angels,

There was a war in heaven between Michael the archangel and his good angels and Satan with his bad angels.

8 And prevailed not; neither was their place found any more in heaven.

Satan and his angels did not win the battle. Additionally, they were not welcome in heaven anymore.

9 And the great dragon was cast out, that old serpent, called the Devil, and Satan, which deceiveth the whole world: he was cast out into the earth, and his angels were cast out with him.

This is repetitious of an earlier verse, but with more detail. The devil who deceives the world especially nonbelievers, was kicked out of heaven with his angels (demons) to earth.

10 And I heard a loud voice saying in heaven, Now is come salvation, and strength, and the kingdom of our God, and the power of his Christ: for the accuser of our brethren is cast down, which accused them before our God day and night.

John heard a loud voice in heaven saying that salvation, strength, the kingdom of God and the power of Christ has come. The accuser of believers is cast down. The devil had accused them before God continuously. The devil never rests in his mission to get mankind to commit sin. 1 Peter Chapter 5 verse 8 states,

Be sober, be vigilant; because your adversary the devil, as a roaring lion, walketh about, seeking whom he may devour:

This is a message to believers. Always watch out for the devil's lies. He wants to devour our faith and strength in Jesus.

11 And they overcame him by the blood of the Lamb, and by the word of their testimony; and they loved not their lives unto the death.

This verse means that believers overcame the devil by the blood of Jesus. In other words, believing that Jesus died on the cross for us. We overcome the devil by our testimony, our faith in Him. We should not be afraid to die for Christ and our faith. Some of us will be beheaded for our faith.

12 Therefore rejoice, *ye* heavens, and ye that dwell in them. Woe to the inhabiters of the earth and of the sea! for the devil is come down unto you, having great wrath, because he knoweth that he hath but a short time.

Those that live in heaven are told to rejoice since the devil isn't up there anymore. They feel sorry for us on earth since he isn't allowed back into heaven. The devil is angry and he knows his time to deceive mankind is very short. The devil knows he is going to hell, but wants as much of mankind with him.

13 And when the dragon saw that he was cast unto the earth, he persecuted the woman which brought forth the man *child*.

The devil, knowing he can't go back to heaven, is causing trouble for the woman (Jerusalem) who brought forth Jesus. We see the city of Jerusalem under attack every day.

14 And to the woman were given two wings of a great eagle, that she might fly into the wilderness, into her place, where she is nourished for a time, and times, and half a time, from the face of the serpent.

This is a repeat of verse 6 with more detail. "Wings" represents protection or assistance in the Bible. Some type of treaty will be signed to allow the rebuilding of the third temple. This is the "confirmed the covenant for a week" from the book of Daniel. The treaty involving the antichrist, is supposed to last longer than three and a half years, but you know, the devil IS a liar!

There are two "wings" or courts that will be in the third temple. An outer court and an inner court. Jerusalem is set upon a mountain. Eagles are known to set their nests in high places. Jerusalem and Mount Zion are referred to as the "wilderness". Remember, Isaiah Chapter 64 verse 10 states,

Thy holy cities are a wilderness, Zion is a wilderness, Jerusalem a desolation.

Moreover, the temple in Jerusalem will be protected from the devil for 3 and a half years (that is the sum of "a time and times and half a time").

15 And the serpent cast out of his mouth water as a flood after the woman, that he might cause her to be carried away of the flood.

Water is symbolic for afflictions (a state of great suffering and distress due to adversity). Isaiah chapter 43 verse 2 states,

When thou passest through the waters, I *will be* with thee; and through the rivers, they shall not overflow thee: when thou walkest through the fire, thou shalt not be burned; neither shall the flame kindle upon thee.

A theory given to me by discernment is from Revelation Chapter 14 verse 6 stating,

And he opened his mouth (the antichrist) **in blasphemy** against God, to blaspheme his name, **and his tabernacle,** and them that dwell in heaven.

The antichrist is blaspheming (using words against) Jerusalem, God, and the temple. He will be causing distress and adversity (affliction). This will arouse the world's hatred to such an elevated degree that it will overflow like a flood to destroy the people and the city. Moreover, the definition of "carry away" in the Merriam-Webster dictionary is, "to arouse to a high and often excessive degree of emotion" (hate/anger).

16 And the earth helped the woman, and the earth opened her mouth, and swallowed up the flood which the dragon cast out of his mouth.

The "earth" will come to the aide of the temple and the city of Jerusalem after hearing the antichrist preaching hatred towards them. By opening its mouth (protests, petitions, and legal battles for the rights of the temple/Jerusalem could work) thereby "swallowing up" the flood of blasphemous words from the antichrist thus helping "the woman" (Jerusalem).

Another theory is, this water could actually be water. Jerusalem has been known to have floods in recent years. For the literal interpretation of Jerusalem being flooded with water, the city of Jerusalem has a sewer system older than 2,000 years. This was the main drainage channel of ancient Jerusalem and the size is huge. This could very well be the earth metaphorically opening her mouth to swallow the flood thus helping the woman.

17 And the dragon was wroth with the woman, and went to make war with the remnant of her seed, which keep the commandments of God, and have the testimony of Jesus Christ.

When the antichrist cannot flood Jerusalem (with words OR water, whichever theory), he becomes very angry it didn't work. The devil will turn his anger towards believers in Christ. Christians have been persecuted since the time of Jesus. It will become worse during the antichrist's reign.

There is a corresponding verse that conveys the message of the antichrist at war with believers.

Revelation Chapter 13 verse 7 states,

And it was given unto him to make war with the saints, and to overcome them: and power was given him over all kindreds, and tongues, and nations.

Additionally, the remnant of the woman is referenced in 2 Kings Chapter 19 verse 31 stating,

For out of Jerusalem shall go forth a remnant, and they that escape out of mount Zion: the zeal of the LORD *of hosts* shall do this.

Chapter 13A

This is Chapter 13 of the book of revelation, but this chapter is similar to Chapter 6, meaning it is hard to describe without including corresponding verses from another book, which is Daniel Chapter 7. After Daniel is cited, Revelation Chapter 13 will be cited. Some verses are self-explanatory. Some verses from Daniel are practically identical to Revelation verses, which is why Daniel Chapter 7 (in its entirety) should be explained first since this book is from the Old Testament and the book of revelation is from the New Testament.

DANIEL CHAPTER 7

1 In the first year of Belshazzar king of Babylon Daniel had a dream and visions of his head upon his bed: then he wrote the dream, *and* told the sum of the matters.

Daniel the prophet had a dream and visions. He wrote down everything he witnessed. This reminds me of John in the book of revelation. Notice the similarities already?

2 Daniel spake and said, I saw in my vision by night, and, behold, the four winds of the heaven strove upon the great sea.

Daniel said he saw visions by night (dreams). He saw the four winds (north, south, east, and west) upon the great sea. The great sea is a metaphor for the nations of the earth.

3 And four great beasts came up from the sea, diverse one from another.

Daniel saw four beasts rising from the sea. Each beast was very different from one another. Each beast represents four kingdoms and men at various times throughout history. These empires had several rulers, but I will only name the reign of the most powerful king based on history and theological consensus.

4 The first *was* like a lion, and had eagle's wings: I beheld till the wings thereof were plucked, and it was lifted up from the earth, and made stand upon the feet as a man, and a man's heart was given to it.

This first empire was the Babylon Empire and King Nebuchadnezzar. This empire was the strongest represented by the lion, king of the beasts. Nebuchadnezzar was the greatest king, but he had too much pride.

God gave the king a dream that only Daniel could interpret. Basically, Daniel told the king that God was displeased with him. He will leave his kingdom and live like the wild animals. He will walk on all fours and eat grass. He will stay that way until his hair grows like the feathers of an eagle. His nails became like claws of a bird. Nebuchadnezzar will live this way for seven years. The king ignored the warning. Everything happened just like Daniel had interpreted.

When the seven years were completed, God had succeeded in humbling Nebuchadnezzar and made him realize that God almighty is the great king above all men. God saw his heart and restored his kingdom.

5 And behold another beast, a second, like to a bear, and it raised up itself on one side, and *it had* three ribs in the mouth of it between the teeth of it: and they said thus unto it, Arise, devour much flesh.

The second empire was the Medo-Persian Empire and Darius I (the empire is also called the Achaemenian Empire). The bear is seen as a powerful predator. The line "it raised itself up on one side" means the Persians were stronger than the Medes. Darius I was the fourth ruler of the Persian Empire. This is mentioned in Daniel Chapter 11 verses 2-3 stating,

And now will I shew thee the truth. Behold, there shall stand up yet three kings in Persia; and the fourth shall be far richer than *they* all: and by his strength through his riches he shall stir up all against the realm of Grecia. And a mighty king shall stand up, that shall rule with great dominion, and do according to his will.

He is referred to as "Darius the Great" because he restored the empire after it was almost destroyed. Within two years, he defeated nine kings in nineteen battles, and as a result, strengthening his empire.

The three ribs in the mouth of "the bear" represent the three main provinces his kingdom ruled over which were Babylon, Lydia, and Egypt. Teeth are represented in the Bible as cruelty. In one battle, a Babylonian, calling himself Nebuchadnezzar IV was trapped with his followers in Babylon. When this battle was over, the city was taken by Darius and his army. Three thousand citizens were crucified as a warning to other potential rebels. I would equate that to cruelty as well as rising up and "devouring much flesh!"

In addition to all of his territorial conquests, early in his reign, Darius was used by God to encourage the Jewish people to complete the building of the second temple.

6 After this I beheld, and lo another, like a leopard, which had upon the back of it four wings of a fowl; the beast had also four heads; and dominion was given to it.

The third beast represents the Greek empire and Alexander the Great.

A leopard refers to the speed of the military conquests of Alexander the Great. The four wings represent the four largest boundaries at the height of his power in 323 BC. These were:

1. The northern boundary The Black Sea and Caspian Sea.
2. The western boundary Macedonia and Greece.
3. The eastern boundary the cities in and around India.
4. The southern boundary went all the way to Libya and Egypt.

After Alexander's death, his empire was divided among five generals, but four became dominant. These became four kingdoms (the four "heads" with dominion).

7 After this I saw in the night visions, and behold a fourth beast, dreadful and terrible, and strong exceedingly; and it had great iron teeth: it devoured and brake in pieces, and stamped the residue with the feet of it: and it *was* diverse from all the beasts that *were* before it; and it had ten horns.

Daniel witnessed in his dream a fourth beast. This beast was very strong. This beast has iron teeth. Remember teeth represent cruelty. Well, iron teeth would mean there will be cruelty on a scale that this world has NEVER seen! This beast is a combination of two kingdoms. The Roman Empire was worldwide and never defeated. The antichrist kingdom shall possess these qualities. The ten horns represent ten "kings" who have given their power and authority to the antichrist. This is how he will make the world submit to him. The word "kings" is in quotations because these men may not hold that actual title, but they have power over nations. Titles may include president, prime minister, etc.

8 I considered the horns, and, behold, there came up among them another little horn, before whom there were three of the first horns plucked up by the roots: and, behold, in this horn *were* eyes like the eyes of man, and a mouth speaking great things.

This little horn represents the false prophet. Horn is a metaphor for king or power. The false prophet has power, but not like the antichrist. He is second in command (actually number three if you count the devil, the antichrist, then him). This man will endorse the antichrist. He is in charge of commanding the world to worship the antichrist and worship his image. Those who do not will be beheaded.

9 I beheld till the thrones were cast down, and the Ancient of days did sit, whose garment *was* white as snow, and the hair of his head like the pure wool: his throne *was like* the fiery flame, *and* his wheels *as* burning fire.

Daniel saw in his dream the throne of God the Father. He was wearing white clothing and his hair was like pure wool. The throne appeared to be as fire.

10 A fiery stream issued and came forth from before him: thousand thousands ministered unto him, and ten thousand times ten thousand stood before him: the judgment was set, and the books were opened.

A stream of fire spewed forth from the throne. (I envision the scene of meeting the wizard from the movie wizard of Oz, but much more frightening)! There were many that ministered to God as well as the 100 million standing before the throne. The books of life were being opened. This event takes place after the 1,000 year reign of Christ. It is discussed in revelation Chapter 20 with greater detail.

11 I beheld then because of the voice of the great words which the horn spake: I beheld *even* till the beast was slain, and his body destroyed, and given to the burning flame.

Daniel saw how much the false prophet praised the antichrist. Daniel watched until the false prophet was defeated; his body was destroyed and cast into the lake of fire.

12 As concerning the rest of the beasts, they had their dominion taken away: yet their lives were prolonged for a season and time.

This goes back to the previously discussed kingdoms. Over time, those kings lost their kingdoms. They had their place in history and fulfilled their purposes.

13 I saw in the night visions, and, behold, *one* like the Son of man came with the clouds of heaven, and came to the Ancient of days, and they brought him near before him.

Daniel saw in his dream, Jesus coming with clouds to the throne of God the Father. Jesus was brought before Him.

14 And there was given him dominion, and glory, and a kingdom, that all people, nations, and languages, should serve him: his dominion *is* an everlasting dominion, which shall not pass away, and his kingdom *that* which shall not be destroyed.

Jesus shall rule over all people from every corner of the earth. He shall be praised. For every knee shall bow and every tongue shall confess that Jesus Christ is Lord! Hallelujah! His kingdom is everlasting and shall NEVER be destroyed.

15 I Daniel was grieved in my spirit in the midst of *my* body, and the visions of my head troubled me.

These visions troubled Daniel. They upset him deeply.

16 I came near unto one of them that stood by, and asked him the truth of all this. So he told me, and made me know the interpretation of the things.

Daniel asked someone standing near him what the meaning of his dream was; the individual explained the interpretation to Daniel.

17 These great beasts, which are four, *are* four kings, *which* shall arise out of the earth.

The great beasts are four kings, which shall arise out of the earth. We know from history, three, the Roman Empire is four, but it is included with the reign of the antichrist. They have already ruled their kingdoms. The antichrist has not ruled his kingdom yet.

18 But the saints of the most High shall take the kingdom, and possess the kingdom for ever, even for ever and ever.

Eventually, at the end of the antichrist's reign of terror, all believers shall rule over the earth WITH Jesus as king for all eternity.

19 Then I would know the truth of the fourth beast, which was diverse from all the others, exceeding dreadful, whose teeth *were of* iron, and his nails *of* brass; *which* devoured, brake in pieces, and stamped the residue with his feet;

The actual fourth beast referred here is the antichrist. Remember, the Roman Empire is mentioned as the fourth kingdom only because of the great worldwide power it held in history. The antichrist kingdom will surpass that power. This verse repeats the power and cruelty he will bring upon mankind.

20 And of the ten horns that *were* in his head, and *of* the other which came up, and before whom three fell; even *of* that horn that had eyes, and a mouth that spake very great things, whose look *was* more stout than his fellows.

This verse restates the power given to the antichrist from the ten "kings" of the earth. The false prophet who has power, but is more "stout" or has slightly less power than the others. He speaks highly of the antichrist.

21 I beheld, and the same horn made war with the saints, and prevailed against them;

The false prophet is in charge of ordering mankind to worship the antichrist and to kill (beheading) all who refuse.

22 Until the Ancient of days came, and judgment was given to the saints of the most High; and the time came that the saints possessed the kingdom.

God the Father and Jesus have been around before the earth was created, so it is appropriate to use the word Ancient to describe them. "Ancient of Days" is found three times in this chapter. Verses 9, 13, and 22. Verse 22 refers to Jesus who will execute God's wrath. In verse 13, the term "ancient of days" is God the Father on His throne and Jesus approaches the throne on clouds. "Ancient of Days" can refer to Jesus Christ and to God the Father.

23 Thus he said, The fourth beast shall be the fourth kingdom upon earth, which shall be diverse from all kingdoms, and shall devour the whole earth, and shall tread it down, and break it in pieces.

The individual told Daniel the fourth beast (the antichrist), although possessing similarities to the other kingdoms, will be different from any kingdom that has ever ruled on earth.

24 And the ten horns out of this kingdom *are* ten kings *that* shall arise: and another shall rise after them; and he shall be diverse from the first, and he shall subdue three kings.

At some point in the future, ten kings will be in power, the antichrist will appear on the scene. He will be different from all men. That's an understatement! He is the son of the devil! The antichrist will conquer three of these kings.

25 And he shall speak *great* words against the most High, and shall wear out the saints of the most High, and think to change times and laws: and they shall be given into his hand until a time and times and the dividing of time.

The antichrist shall blaspheme the name of God and kill believers. He will change the way we live by changing laws. Mankind (believers will be under his rule for three and a half years, seven for nonbelievers). This is the part of the future I dread. Whether I'm alive or not when it happens, I have great sympathy for the believers who will be alive during that time.

26 But the judgment shall sit, and they shall take away his dominion, to consume and to destroy *it* unto the end.

God (Jesus AND the Father) shall judge the antichrist. They will take away his power and destroy it! Hallelujah!

27 And the kingdom and dominion, and the greatness of the kingdom under the whole heaven, shall be given to the people of the saints of the most High, whose kingdom *is* an everlasting kingdom, and all dominions shall serve and obey him.

The kingdoms of this earth will be given to Jesus and His believers forever. Believers shall gladly serve and obey Jesus Christ. I think of this as treating loving parents with respect. If we can serve and obey those who have lovingly raised us, we should DEFINITELY be able to love, serve, and obey the One who saved us from the torment of eternal hell!

28 Hitherto *is* the end of the matter. As for me Daniel, my cogitations much troubled me, and my countenance changed in me: but I kept the matter in my heart.

This is the end of Daniel's dream. His visions continue to perplex him so much that it causes his mood to change, but his feelings remain hidden.

Chapter 13B

1 And I stood upon the sand of the sea, and saw a beast rise up out of the sea, having seven heads and ten horns, and upon his horns ten crowns, and upon his heads the name of blasphemy.

Sand of the sea is used to represent multitudes of people. This is referenced in Revelation Chapter 20 verse 8 stating,

And shall go out to deceive the nations which are in the four quarters of the earth, Gog and Magog, to gather them together to battle: the number of whom *is* as the sand of the sea. The sea represents political and military power. He has seven heads, which are seven kingdoms. He has ten horns, which are kings, hence the ten crowns. At some point in time, these earthly kings shall freely give the beast their "crowns" or power over their respective nations.

2 And the beast which I saw was like unto a leopard, and his feet were as *the feet* of a bear, and his mouth as the mouth of a lion: and the dragon gave him his power, and his seat, and great authority.

Remember Daniel Chapter 7? This verse is why that was covered extensively to make sense of the animal characteristics attributed to the antichrist. The leopard is the Greek Empire of Alexander the Great, who conquered the world with the speed of a leopard. It is said that Alexander cried when told by his generals there was no one left to conquer. The bear is the Medo-Persian Empire. The lion is the Babylonian Empire. The dragon is the devil who gives the beast his supernatural power and control over the earth.

3 And I saw one of his heads as it were wounded to death; and his deadly wound was healed: and all the world wondered after the beast.

At some point in time, the beast is mortally wounded and dies from his injuries. The wound heals and He comes back to life (and no, not like a zombie, like a "normal" looking human being). Although the antichrist will appear human, he is not human. He is said to be born of the devil. This verse is a blasphemous replication of Jesus death, burial, and resurrection. The beast is so unoriginal! A pure copycat! Of course, if the whole world witnessed a resurrection, it would cause people to "wonder after the beast."

4 And they worshipped the dragon which gave power unto the beast: and they worshipped the beast, saying, Who *is* like unto the beast? who is able to make war with him?

Currently, many people worship the devil. This will increase exponentially after the antichrist is raised from the dead "performance." Non-believers will say, who on earth is like this man? Who will be able to fight against his powers? Jesus Christ can and will. Amen to the Lamb of God!

5 And there was given unto him a mouth speaking great things and blasphemies; and power was given unto him to continue forty *and* two months.

The antichrist knows how to speak eloquently regarding human issues as well as against God.

6 And he opened his mouth in blasphemy against God, to blaspheme his name, and his tabernacle, and them that dwell in heaven.

The antichrist speaks against everything associated with God. This is the verbal "flood" referred to in Chapter 12 since the tabernacle of God will be in Jerusalem.

7 And it was given unto him to make war with the saints, and to overcome them: and power was given him over all kindreds, and tongues, and nations.

Just like Chapter 12, when the antichrist cannot convince the world to hate God including Jerusalem, he will set his evil sights upon all believers in Christ. He will try to kill (beheading being the preferred manner) all of them before they are caught up in the clouds by Jesus (the rapture). The antichrist will control the entire earth.

8 And all that dwell upon the earth shall worship him, whose names are not written in the book of life of the Lamb slain from the foundation of the world.

All non-believers will worship the antichrist. Additionally, this verse means, if you worship him, his image, or take his mark in your hand or forehead, you will be damned for eternity! This verse scares me. Being damned (going to hell) for eternity is NOT on my bucket list.

9 If any man have an ear, let him hear.

God is warning ALL OF MANKIND with this verse. If ANY man who has ears (the capacity to understand) LISTEN! God is warning you of the future and He wants mankind to choose eternity with Him.

10 He that leadeth into captivity shall go into captivity: he that killeth with the sword must be killed with the sword. Here is the patience and the faith of the saints.

Unfortunately, this verse is for the believers (saints, Christians) that will be here during the tribulation (not wrath of God). This is why it is stated that the saints must have patience and faith in Jesus, to wait for His return. Moreover, God is telling us everyone will get what they deserve in the end. Wicked or righteous, you will receive your reward.

11 And I beheld another beast coming up out of the earth; and he had two horns like a lamb, and he spake as a dragon.

John observes another "beast" coming up out of the earth. This is a man, a human man. All humans are "dust from the earth." Remember Adam, the first man? This man (the false prophet) appears to be kind and merciful, but is as evil as the devil himself. This man is believed to be the pope (whoever that will be at the time of the antichrist's reign). The two horns are his kingdoms (theological and political).

12 And he exerciseth all the power of the first beast before him, and causeth the earth and them which dwell therein to worship the first beast, whose deadly wound was healed.

This man has supernatural powers like the antichrist. He will publicly endorse and campaign for mankind to worship the antichrist.

13 And he doeth great wonders, so that he maketh fire come down from heaven on the earth in the sight of men,

He can perform "wonders." This reminds me of the Ten Commandments when the magicians/priests in the court of pharaoh turned their sticks into snakes as Moses did, but Moses' miracle was the power of God. Pharaoh's miracle was from the devil, just as this man's power. In 2 Corinthians Chapter 11 verses 13-15 states,

For such *are* false apostles, deceitful workers, transforming themselves into the apostles of Christ.
And no marvel; for Satan himself is transformed into an angel of light.

Therefore *it is* no great thing if his ministers also be transformed as the ministers of righteousness; whose end shall be according to their works.
For pretending to be working for God, they will get what is coming to them.

And deceiveth them that dwell on the earth by *the means of* those miracles which he had power to do in the sight of the beast; saying to them that dwell on the earth, that they should make an image to the beast, which had the wound by a sword, and did live.

The false prophet will convince most of mankind into believing this is Christ by performing miracles and signs of wonder. He will campaign for an image of the beast to be erected since the beast was dead and has been brought back to life; he will say he is worthy enough to be praised. The real Lamb of God, Jesus Christ is the only one worthy to be praised! He died and rose again from the dead to give mankind an opportunity to live forever in the new heaven and new earth for eternity. This false Christ only wants praise! It's all about him! Narcissist! The only reward you will receive from worshipping and following him is death, hell, and eternal torment!

15 And he had power to give life unto the image of the beast, that the image of the beast should both speak, and cause that as many as would not worship the image of the beast should be killed.

The false prophet has the ability to bring this image of the antichrist to life (pharaoh magician). The image will be able to talk. Many people will be killed if they do not worship this image. I'm ready! My faith is in these scriptures. Matthew Chapter 10 verse 28 states,

And fear not them which kill the body, but are not able to kill the soul: but rather fear him which is able to destroy both soul and body in hell.

And also in Luke Chapter 12 verse 4 states,

And I say unto you my friends, Be not afraid of them that kill the body, and after that have no more that they can do.

16 And he causeth all, both small and great, rich and poor, free and bond, to receive a mark in their right hand, or in their foreheads:

The antichrist and the false prophet will try to make every human being take the mark of the beast either in the right hand or forehead.

17 And that no man might buy or sell, save he that had the mark, or the name of the beast, or the number of his name.

Without this mark, the name of the beast, or the number of his name, no one on earth can buy or sell anything.

18 Here is wisdom. Let him that hath understanding count the number of the beast: for it is the number of a man; and his number *is* Six hundred threescore *and* six.

The antichrist number is 666. Remember, if you don't worship the beast, take His mark, take his name, or number, you will be killed. Most likely beheaded. That is why "beheaded" is the title of this book. As a young Christian, I was terrified of this and prayed that God would spare ALL BELIEVERS. He will not. The reason, I believe is that some Christians need to have their faith challenged to the point of no return, like those "lukewarm" Christians at the church of Laodicea.

Anyone who is threatened to be beheaded for Jesus, will know just how strong their faith is in Him! Hallelujah!

Chapter 14

1 And I looked, and, lo, a Lamb stood on the mount Zion, and with him an hundred forty *and* four thousand, having his Father's name written in their foreheads.

John observes Jesus standing on Mount Zion with the 144,000 of men from all 12 tribes. These are not the 144,000 "Jews" as they are commonly referred to by individuals. Remember, it is important to note the difference between these two nations: Israel and Judah. While all people living there were Israelites because they were descendants of Jacob (Israel), not all Israelites were Jews. Some Israelites came from tribes other than Judah and Benjamin. Additionally, the first time the word, *Jew,* appears in the Bible, the nations of Israel and Syria are at war with the "Jews."

2 And I heard a voice from heaven, as the voice of many waters, and as the voice of a great thunder: and I heard the voice of harpers harping with their harps:

John heard a voice from heaven that sounded like many waters and thunder. He heard singing and harps playing.

3 And they sung as it were a new song before the throne, and before the four beasts, and the elders: and no man could learn that song but the hundred *and* forty *and* four thousand, which were redeemed from the earth.

These harpers sung a new song before the throne of God. The only individuals that could learn this new song was the 144,000.

4 These are they which were not defiled with women; for they are virgins. These are they which follow the Lamb whithersoever he goeth. These were redeemed from among men, *being* the first fruits unto God and to the Lamb.

This verse proves the gender of the entire 144,000. They are men who were not "defiled" with women, they are virgins. They follow Jesus wherever He goes and were redeemed from mankind unto God the Father and Jesus.

5 And in their mouth was found no guile: for they are without fault before the throne of God.

Their speech was gentle and innocent. They were pure in their hearts, mind, body and soul.

6 And I saw another angel fly in the midst of heaven, having the everlasting gospel to preach unto them that dwell on the earth, and to every nation, and kindred, and tongue, and people,

John saw an angel flying around heaven. This angel had the everlasting gospel for all of mankind.

7 Saying with a loud voice, Fear God, and give glory to him; for the hour of his judgment is come: and worship him that made heaven, and earth, and the sea, and the fountains of waters.

This angel proclaimed loudly for us to fear God and give Him glory. Worship Him because He made heaven, earth, and all the water. God is about to pour out His wrath upon the earth.

8 And there followed another angel, saying, Babylon is fallen, is fallen, that great city, because she made all nations drink of the wine of the wrath of her fornication.

John saw another angel saying that Babylon has fallen, which is a great city (Jerusalem). Babylon is symbolic for man's system of rules orchestrated by the devil. Remember when Jesus spoke about the synagogue of Satan and those who do not believe in Jesus are as the antichrist (against God)? This is why. When the third temple is built and daily sacrifices resume, this is considered blasphemy. Jesus said it is finished! He was the last sacrificial Lamb. He came to fulfill the law with His birth, death, and resurrection.

This metaphorical "she" is not married to Christ, therefore she has committed fornication. Fornication represents idol worship. Judaism has believers all over the world (all nations). The entire world (non-believers) will drink the wine of the wrath (the wrath of God).

9 And the third angel followed them, saying with a loud voice, If any man worship the beast and his image, and receive *his* mark in his forehead, or in his hand,

A third angel followed after the other angels, proclaiming loudly that if anyone worships the beast in any manner, they will face the wrath of God.

10 The same shall drink of the wine of the wrath of God, which is poured out without mixture into the cup of his indignation; and he shall be tormented with fire and brimstone in the presence of the holy angels, and in the presence of the Lamb:

If you worship the beast in any manner, you will be damned, destined to go straight to hell! If you blindly follow the laws of this world, you can be forgiven. All you have to do is ask for forgiveness (repent) but if you worship the beast, you cannot ask for forgiveness.

11 And the smoke of their torment ascendeth up for ever and ever: and they have no rest day nor night, who worship the beast and his image, and whosoever receiveth the mark of his name.

The damned will be tormented and the smoke of their torment shall rise up forever. They will never rest for all eternity. Yeah, I'd rather have my head chopped off any day than to face eternal torment! As previously stated in the last chapter, after death, the torment is over!

12 Here is the patience of the saints: here *are* they that keep the commandments of God, and the faith of Jesus.

Believers should have patience, STRONG faith, and keep the commandments (as humanly possible) but the biggest command in this setting is NOT to worship the beast.

13 And I heard a voice from heaven saying unto me, Write, Blessed *are* the dead which die in the Lord from henceforth: Yea, saith the Spirit, that they may rest from their labours; and their works do follow them.

John heard a voice from heaven telling him to write that all believers from this moment on (from John's time until the return of Jesus) are blessed. The spirit added, they will be given rest from labor and the good deeds they have done in the name of God will follow them.

14 And I looked, and behold a white cloud, and upon the cloud *one* sat like unto the Son of man, having on his head a golden crown, and in his hand a sharp sickle.

John saw Jesus sitting on a cloud with a gold crown on His head. Jesus held a sharp sickle. He is coming for His followers.

15 And another angel came out of the temple, crying with a loud voice to him that sat on the cloud, Thrust in thy sickle, and reap: for the time is come for thee to reap; for the harvest of the earth is ripe.

John observed another angel coming out of the temple proclaiming loudly to Jesus for Him to thrust His sickle into the earth and reap the harvest of believers. The time has come for them to be separated from the grapes (the wicked, non-believers). This is the "rapture".

16 And he that sat on the cloud thrust in his sickle on the earth; and the earth was reaped.

Jesus came to earth on a cloud (just as He left) thrust His sickle into the earth and gathered the righteous.

17 And another angel came out of the temple which is in heaven, he also having a sharp sickle.

John observed another angel come out of the temple with another sickle.

18 And another angel came out from the altar, which had power over fire; and cried with a loud cry to him that had the sharp sickle, saying, Thrust in thy sharp sickle, and gather the clusters of the vine of the earth; for her grapes are fully ripe.

Another angel came out of the temple, who had the power of fire. He proclaimed loudly to the angel with the sharp sickle for him to thrust his sickle into the earth. They are gathering the grapes from the vine of the earth. These are the wicked (non-believers). Deuteronomy Chapter 32-33 states,

For their vine *is* of the vine of Sodom, and of the fields of Gomorrah: their grapes *are* grapes of gall, their clusters *are* bitter:
Their wine *is* the poison of dragons, and the cruel venom of asps.

19 And the angel thrust in his sickle into the earth, and gathered the vine of the earth, and cast *it* into the great winepress of the wrath of God.

The angel thrust his sickle into the earth, gathered the vine, and threw it into the wine press. This is all metaphorical imagery. The non-believers are not actually grapes that are going into a wine press, but when the wrath of God begins, there will be great bloodshed.

20 And the winepress was trodden without the city, and blood came out of the winepress, even unto the horse bridles, by the space of a thousand *and* six hundred furlongs.

The people were punished without punishing the city (yet). The blood pours out of the wine press. There is so much blood that it rises as high as a horses bridle. A furlong is approximately $1/8^{th}$ of a mile in modern terms. Using that calculation, that's 200 miles of blood! God is mad! Regardless of what metaphor is used (wheat or clusters of grapes) the wicked are being gathered together for judgment. They have been marked and identified by receiving the mark of the beast. I find it poetic justice that the beast and the false prophet use the mark to martyr believers who refuse to receive it and Jesus, upon His return, uses that very same mark to identify who will remain on earth to face the wrath of God. Glory to the Lamb of God!

Chapter 15

1 And I saw another sign in heaven, great and marvelous, seven angels having the seven last plagues; for in them is filled up the wrath of God.

John observes seven angels holding seven plagues, which is the wrath of God to be poured out upon the non-believers on earth.

2 And I saw as it were a sea of glass mingled with fire: and them that had gotten the victory over the beast, and over his image, and over his mark, *and* over the number of his name, stand on the sea of glass, having the harps of God.

John observes the martyrs (Christians) who were killed for not worshipping the beast, his image, nor the mark of the beast.
This verse is the definitive verse that should put an end to the controversy about Christians being here on earth during the TRIBULATION! Christians that are alive in the world during the reign of the antichrist will go through the tribulation. That is how they will get victory over the beast, his image and his mark; by being killed for refusing to accept these things. The Christians will be standing in heaven holding harps of God.

3 And they sing the song of Moses the servant of God, and the song of the Lamb, saying, Great and marvelous *are* thy works, Lord God Almighty; just and true *are* thy ways, thou King of saints.

The believers sing songs of praise to God the Father and to Jesus.

4 Who shall not fear thee, O Lord, and glorify thy name? for *thou* only *art* holy: for all nations shall come and worship before thee; for thy judgments are made manifest.

They ask who shall fear (have reverence) for Jesus and glorify His name. Jesus is Holy. All of mankind shall bow a knee and every tongue shall confess that Jesus Christ is Lord. For He will execute the wrath of God!

5 And after that I looked, and, behold, the temple of the tabernacle of the testimony in heaven was opened:

John saw the temple of testimony in heaven open.

6 And the seven angels came out of the temple, having the seven plagues, clothed in pure and white linen, and having their breasts girded with golden girdles.

John observed seven angels coming out of the temple dressed in pure white linen with golden girdles around their chests each carrying a plague.

7 And one of the four beasts gave unto the seven angels seven golden vials full of the wrath of God, who liveth for ever and ever.

One of the four beasts gave each of the seven angels a golden vial filled with the wrath of God. Remember the seven trumpets? These are the seven vials that are poured out upon the earth AT THE SAME TIME as the trumpets. There are some individuals who believe just because we read about the seven trumpets first that the vials come AFTER the trumpets. This is the same story and timeline as earlier, just told with additional detail.

8 And the temple was filled with smoke from the glory of God, and from his power; and no man was able to enter into the temple, till the seven plagues of the seven angels were fulfilled.

The heavenly temple was filled with smoke from the glory and power of God. No man could go inside of the temple until God had finished pouring out His wrath upon the earth. God is showing unbelievers that He is real and He is in charge.

Chapter 16

1 And I heard a great voice out of the temple saying to the seven angels, Go your ways, and pour out the vials of the wrath of God upon the earth.

God tells the seven angels to pour the vials upon the earth. This is done one at a time, in order.

2 And the first went, and poured out his vial upon the earth; and there fell a noisome and grievous sore upon the men which had the mark of the beast, and *upon* them which worshipped his image.

When the first angel poured out his vial, everyone who had taken the mark and worshipped the beast became covered in painful sores.

Remember Revelation Chapter 8 verse 7 states,

The first angel sounded, and there followed hail and fire mingled with blood, and they were cast upon the earth: and the third part of trees was burnt up, and all green grass was burnt up.

The first trumpet brought fire and the first vial brought painful sores.

3 And the second angel poured out his vial upon the sea; and it became as the blood of a dead *man*: and every living soul died in the sea.

The second angel poured out his vial upon the sea and turned it to blood. Everything in the sea died. Revelation Chapter 8 verses 8-9 states,

And the second angel sounded, and as it were a great mountain burning with fire was cast into the sea: and the third part of the sea became blood;
And the third part of the creatures which were in the sea, and had life, died; and the third part of the ships were destroyed.

The second trumpet and second vial involve turning the sea to blood and killing sea life as well as destroying ships.

4 And the third angel poured out his vial upon the rivers and fountains of waters; and they became blood.

The third angel poured out his vial. The rivers and fountains became blood. Revelation Chapter 8 verse 10-11 states,
And the third angel sounded, and there fell a great star from heaven, burning as it were a lamp, and it fell upon the third part of the rivers, and upon the fountains of waters;
And the name of the star is called Wormwood: and the third part of the waters became wormwood; and many men died of the waters, because they were made bitter.

The third trumpet and the third vial turned the smaller bodies of water bitter or to blood.

5 And I heard the angel of the waters say, Thou art righteous, O Lord, which art, and wast, and shalt be, because thou hast judged thus.

The angel in control of the water praised Jesus by calling Him righteous and praised His judgments upon the water of the earth.

6 For they have shed the blood of saints and prophets, and thou hast given them blood to drink; for they are worthy.

This angel states because the wicked have shed so much innocent blood of saints and prophets throughout history, they should drink blood. They deserve it.

7 And I heard another out of the altar say, Even so, Lord God Almighty, true and righteous *are* thy judgments.

John heard someone by the throne say regardless if the wicked deserve it, the judgment and wrath of God are true and righteous.

8 And the fourth angel poured out his vial upon the sun; and power was given unto him to scorch men with fire.

The fourth angel poured out his vial on the sun. The earth became hot as fire. Revelation Chapter 8 verse 12 states,

And the fourth angel sounded, and the third part of the sun was smitten, and the third part of the moon, and the third part of the stars; so as the third part of them were darkened, and the day shone not for a third part of it, and the night likewise. Apparently, the part of the sun that still shone was extremely hot.

The fourth trumpet and fourth vial causes the sun, moon and stars to either darkened or create intense heat.

9 And men were scorched with great heat, and blasphemed the name of God, which hath power over these plagues: and they repented not to give him glory.

As the wicked are being burned with this intense heat, they curse God. God has power over the plagues, and instead of giving Him credit for being able to cause such destruction and pain, they will not ask for forgiveness. Evil to the core.

10 And the fifth angel poured out his vial upon the seat of the beast; and his kingdom was full of darkness; and they gnawed their tongues for pain,

The fifth angel poured out his vial on the kingdom of the beast (which is the entire earth). Revelation Chapter 9 verses 1-6 states,

And the fifth angel sounded, and I saw a star fall from heaven unto the earth: and to him was given the key of the bottomless pit.
And he opened the bottomless pit; and there arose a smoke out of the pit, as the smoke of a great furnace; and the sun and the air were darkened by reason of the smoke of the pit.
And there came out of the smoke locusts upon the earth: and unto them was given power, as the scorpions of the earth have power.
And it was commanded them that they should not hurt the grass of the earth, neither any green thing, neither any tree; but only those men which have not the seal of God in their foreheads.
And to them it was given that they should not kill them, but that they should be tormented five months: and their torment *was* as the torment of a scorpion, when he striketh a man.
And in those days shall men seek death, and shall not find it; and shall desire to die, and death shall flee from them.

The fifth trumpet brings darkness and locusts that sting like scorpions for FIVE months. The fifth vial brings darkness and pain. The pain is from the scorpion stings and the sores covering their bodies. The only people on earth not being stung are the two witnesses and the 144,000. They have the seal of God in their foreheads as protection.

11 And blasphemed the God of heaven because of their pains and their sores, and repented not of their deeds.

The wicked still refuse to ask for forgiveness and repent despite the pain and sores. I would beg God to forgive me daily!

12 And the sixth angel poured out his vial upon the great river Euphrates; and the water thereof was dried up, that the way of the kings of the east might be prepared.

The sixth angel poured out his vial upon the river Euphrates. This caused the river to dry up, to make way for the battle of Armageddon.
Revelation Chapter 9 verses 13-15 states,

And the sixth angel sounded, and I heard a voice from the four horns of the golden altar which is before God,
Saying to the sixth angel which had the trumpet, Loose the four angels which are bound in the great river Euphrates.
And the four angels were loosed, which were prepared for an hour, and a day, and a month, and a year, for to slay the third part of men.

The fifth trumpet and the fifth vial both involve the Euphrates River becoming dry. This releases the four angels guarding the tree of life to kill a third of mankind and creates a pathway of accessibility to the battle of Armageddon.

13 And I saw three unclean spirits like frogs *come* out of the mouth of the dragon, and out of the mouth of the beast, and out of the mouth of the false prophet.

Demons are released from the mouth of the devil, the antichrist, and the false prophet.

14 For they are the spirits of devils, working miracles, *which* go forth unto the kings of the earth and of the whole world, to gather them to the battle of that great day of God Almighty.

These are spirits (demons) helping the "unholy trinity" by going to the kings of the earth and convincing them Jesus is an enemy that they need to fight.

15 Behold, I come as a thief. Blessed *is* he that watcheth, and keepeth his garments, lest he walk naked, and they see his shame.

This verse is directed to believers and anyone who reads revelation (and this book)! Jesus is stating that He will come as a thief upon anyone who does not know about the warnings of revelation. Believers should know what to expect as these events take place so they will not be embarrassed. In other words, as a Christian, you should be ashamed of yourself if you do not read AND understand the book of revelation. This is another reason I wrote this book. I wanted as many people as possible to read it and understand what is going to happen on earth very soon.

16 And he gathered them together into a place called in the Hebrew tongue Armageddon.

The antichrist, devil, and false prophet gathered the kings along with their armies for the battle of Armageddon.

17 And the seventh angel poured out his vial into the air; and there came a great voice out of the temple of heaven, from the throne, saying, It is done.

The seventh angel poured out his vial into the air. There was a great voice (God the Father) coming out of the heavenly temple stating the wrath of God is complete. Revelation Chapter 11 verse 15 states,

And the seventh angel sounded; and there were great voices in heaven, saying, The kingdoms of this world are become *the kingdoms* of our Lord, and of his Christ; and he shall reign for ever and ever.

Both verses state when the seventh trumpet is blown and the seventh vial is poured out, the wrath of God is over. The kingdoms on earth now belong to Jesus Christ our Lord. Technically, those in heaven are rejoicing before the last plagues (trumpet and vial) are performed. They are so happy; they have gotten ahead of the events. Note: these judgments were upon the wicked. God has not judged the cities, but the seventh trumpet and vial will start their punishment.

18 And there were voices, and thunders, and lightnings; and there was a great earthquake, such as was not since men were upon the earth, so mighty an earthquake, *and* so great.

In heaven, there were voices with thunder and lightning. John observes the biggest earthquake in the history of mankind.
Revelation Chapter 11 verse 19 states,

And the temple of God was opened in heaven, and there was seen in his temple the ark of his testament: and there were lightnings, and voices, and thunderings, and an earthquake, and great hail.

19 And the great city was divided into three parts, and the cities of the nations fell: and great Babylon came in remembrance before God, to give unto her the cup of the wine of the fierceness of his wrath.

Jerusalem was divided into three parts. Cities throughout the world fell. Babylon (man's idolatry and rules) were remembered by God, which caused Him to shake this earth with great force.

20 And every island fled away, and the mountains were not found.

The force of the earthquake was so hard it caused islands to be moved out of their places and there were no more mountains. That is powerful.

21 And there fell upon men a great hail out of heaven, *every stone* about the weight of a talent: and men blasphemed God because of the plague of the hail; for the plague thereof was exceeding great.

The "great hail" mentioned in revelation Chapter 11 verse 19, was the weight of a talent. A talent weighs about 60 pounds! Can you imagine that? Can you picture the destruction to houses, cars, and people, if 60 pounds fell out of the sky?

Men blasphemed God because of the hail. Of course, the wicked is cursing God. They refuse to repent after all of this! "For the plague thereof was exceedingly great." Exceedingly great is an understatement! God is almighty and extremely mad at the wicked.

Chapter 17

1 And there came one of the seven angels which had the seven vials, and talked with me, saying unto me, Come hither; I will shew unto thee the judgment of the great whore that sitteth upon many waters:

John encounters the angel who held the seven vials. The angel told John that he wanted to show him the judgment of the great whore. There has been much debate about who is the whore. Once upon a time (very recently) I believed it was the papal system (Catholics) in Rome. It is not, it is the city of Jerusalem. Follow as I explain.

2 With whom the kings of the earth have committed fornication, and the inhabitants of the earth have been made drunk with the wine of her fornication.

Fornication can be defined as having sex without being married. Symbolically, it means idolatry. Jerusalem, throughout history, has been known for practicing idolatry. The rulers who have conquered Jerusalem throughout the centuries have brought their pagan gods with them. Judaism is a form of idolatry (remember the synagogue of Satan?) for having rejected the messiah.

3 So he carried me away in the spirit into the wilderness: and I saw a woman sit upon a scarlet coloured beast, full of names of blasphemy, having seven heads and ten horns.

The angel carries John into the wilderness. Remember in revelation Chapter 12, I pointed out that the tabernacle of God was in the wilderness. The woman (Jerusalem) is sitting on the beast (the antichrist). He has his seven heads (which are kingdoms) and ten horns (ten kings who are not in power at this point in history). Jerusalem is guilty of forming an alliance with the Romans who were in control of the city at that time. This alliance aided in the crucifixion of Jesus.

4 And the woman was arrayed in purple and scarlet colour, and decked with gold and precious stones and pearls, having a golden cup in her hand full of abominations and filthiness of her fornication:

The woman (Jerusalem) is wearing colors associated with the veil in the temple. Exodus Chapter 26 verse 1 states,
Moreover thou shalt make the tabernacle *with* ten curtains *of* fine twined linen, and blue, and purple, and scarlet: *with* cherubims of cunning work shalt thou make them.

For the precious stones, 2 Chronicles Chapter 3 verses 1 and 6 state,

Then Solomon began to build the house of the LORD at Jerusalem in mount Moriah, where *the LORD* appeared unto David his father, in the place that David had prepared in the threshing floor of Ornan the Jebusite.
And he garnished the house with precious stones for beauty: and the gold *was* gold of Parvaim.

Additionally, women wore pearls as a sign of wealth. Regarding the golden cup, a cup was often used during idol worship.

5 And upon her forehead *was* a name written, MYSTERY, BABYLON THE GREAT, THE MOTHER OF HARLOTS AND ABOMINATIONS OF THE EARTH.

There were many pagan rituals that contained mysteries or secrets that were shared with members only. Think of secret initiations. Babylon was known for its extensive idol worship. It became known as the birthplace of pagan worship, the "mother of harlots and abominations of the earth" as its influence spread throughout the world.

6 And I saw the woman drunken with the blood of the saints, and with the blood of the martyrs of Jesus: and when I saw her, I wondered with great admiration.

Although there are many instances in the Bible that fit this verse, the one that stands out is the infamous Jezebel. Despite being the queen of Jerusalem, she practiced idol worship. She had at least 850 pagan prophets at her service. She forced her pagan beliefs onto those who feared the one true God. Her method of dealing with those who opposed her was simple, she killed them. The prophet Elijah had to leave Jerusalem because he killed hundreds of her prophets. This, of course, made her angry enough to threaten his life. Ironically, it was Elijah who prophesied her horrible death. Her husband, Ahab (the king of Jerusalem) was unaware of her evil deeds.

The fact that Jezebel is a literal female and the city of Jerusalem is a symbolic female makes her story and this verse fit perfectly together.

7 And the angel said unto me, Wherefore didst thou marvel? I will tell thee the mystery of the woman, and of the beast that carrieth her, which hath the seven heads and ten horns.

The angel asked John why he was so perplexed. The angel told John he will explain what he observed and the participants.

8 The beast that thou sawest was, and is not; and shall ascend out of the bottomless pit, and go into perdition: and they that dwell on the earth shall wonder, whose names were not written in the book of life from the foundation of the world, when they behold the beast that was, and is not, and yet is.

The beast the angel mentions is the antichrist. He shall ascend out from hell and wreak havoc upon the earth. Those individuals alive at this time, especially non-believers, will be in awe of the antichrist living, then dying, and ultimately rising from the dead (like a false Jesus). Although believers will be in awe (I know I would!) they will know the truth for having understood the book of revelation. It is important to understand revelation, so you will not be fascinated by the antichrist's parlor tricks!

9 And here *is* the mind which hath wisdom. The seven heads are seven mountains, on which the woman sitteth.

Although Jerusalem is sitting among seven literal mountains, (as referred to in the book of Enoch), this is not what is being conveyed in this verse. Mountains represent kingdoms. These are the kingdoms that have conquered Jerusalem throughout history.

10 And there are seven kings: five are fallen, and one is, *and* the other is not yet come; and when he cometh, he must continue a short space.

Remember in Revelation Chapter 13, we discussed Daniel Chapter 7 as well? This verse is referring to those kingdoms but starts with Egypt. The book of Daniel starts with the Babylonian empire because his visions started at that point in time. Since this is revelation and later in history, John can go to the past AND future.

The five fallen are: **Egypt, Assyria, Babylon, Medo-Persia**, and **Greece.** The kingdom at the time revelation was written is **Rome.** Remember Rome was never conquered and neither will the kingdom of the antichrist. Technically, it will be conquered by God.

11 And the beast that was, and is not, even he is the eighth, and is of the seven, and goeth into perdition.

Actually, the antichrist is the eighth "king" or ruler who receives his power from the seventh king, his father, the devil.

12 And the ten horns which thou sawest are ten kings, which have received no kingdom as yet; but receive power as kings one hour with the beast.

These kings were covered several times in earlier chapters. To repeat, they are rulers who will turn over their power and authority to the antichrist. They do not rule over their kingdoms yet, but will in the near future. Remember Daniel Chapter 7 verses 7-8 stating,

After this I saw in the night visions, and behold a fourth beast, dreadful and terrible, and strong exceedingly; and it had great iron teeth: it devoured and brake in pieces, and stamped the residue with the feet of it: and it *was* diverse from all the beasts that *were* before it; and it had ten horns.
I considered the horns, and, behold, there came up among them another little horn, before whom there were three of the first horns plucked up by the roots: and, behold, in this horn *were* eyes like the eyes of man, and a mouth speaking great things.

This happened when the Roman Empire, although never conquered, but was divided up by ten barbarian tribes. Around this time, the pope became politically prominent along with the Roman Catholic Church. Three of the barbarian tribes did not agree with the church, so they were "plucked up by the roots". What happens to something plucked up by the roots? It dies. The little horn (the pope) destroyed the three "horns". History is going to repeat itself during the rise of the antichrist.

13 These have one mind, and shall give their power and strength unto the beast.

The rulers give up everything to be controlled by the antichrist.

14 These shall make war with the Lamb, and the Lamb shall overcome them: for he is Lord of lords, and King of kings: and they that are with him *are called*, and chosen, and faithful.

This verse is referring to the battle of Armageddon. Jesus will defeat all of them. Believers are called by Him, chosen by Him, and remain faithful to Him.

15 And he saith unto me, The waters which thou sawest, where the whore sitteth, are peoples, and multitudes, and nations, and tongues.

There isn't a nation in the world that hasn't heard of nor isn't influenced by the city of Jerusalem.

16 And the ten horns which thou sawest upon the beast, these shall hate the whore, and shall make her desolate and naked, and shall eat her flesh, and burn her with fire.

The book of Ezekiel mentions punishment for Jerusalem's abomination. Ezekiel Chapter 16 verse 2 states (as proof God is referring to Jerusalem)

Son of man (Jesus), cause Jerusalem to know her abominations.

Ezekiel Chapter 16 verses 35-41 continues stating,

Wherefore, O harlot, hear the word of the LORD:
Thus saith the Lord GOD; Because thy filthiness was poured out, and thy nakedness discovered through thy whoredoms with thy lovers, and with all the idols of thy abominations, and by the blood of thy children, which thou didst give unto them;
Behold, therefore I will gather all thy lovers, with whom thou hast taken pleasure, and all *them* that thou hast loved, with all *them* that thou hast hated; I will even gather them round about against thee, and will discover thy

nakedness unto them, that they may see all thy nakedness.

And I will judge thee, as women that break wedlock and shed blood are judged; and I will give thee blood in fury and jealousy.

And I will also give thee into their hand, and they shall throw down thine eminent place, and shall break down thy high places: they shall strip thee also of thy clothes, and shall take thy fair jewels, and leave thee naked and bare.

They shall also bring up a company against thee, and they shall stone thee with stones, and thrust thee through with their swords.

And they shall burn thine houses with fire, and execute judgments upon thee in the sight of many women: and I will cause thee to cease from playing the harlot, and thou also shalt give no hire any more.

We see from the Old Testament, God is angry at Jerusalem for worshipping pagan idols from her "lovers" (kingdoms who conquered her). She is naked because she doesn't have the covering of God's covenant over her. He threatens her saying He will gather her "lovers" (the kingdoms) and cause them to see she is no longer covered by the covenant of God. They will riot and burn her with fire. Just like He is doing here in the book of revelation. God was angry then and He is just as angry now (and will be when this takes place).

17 For God hath put in their hearts to fulfil his will, and to agree, and give their kingdom unto the beast, until the words of God shall be fulfilled.

God the Father is in full control of all events. It is He who ALLOWS the rulers to accomplish the will of the antichrist, to give up their power until God says He is done playing this "game."

18 And the woman which thou sawest is that great city, which reigneth over the kings of the earth.

The woman is Jerusalem. The city "reigns" over the kings of the earth. Definition of the word reign: dominance, prevalence, or sway. The definition of prevalence: The quality or condition of being prevalent or influence. The definition of influence: A power affecting a person, thing, or course of events, especially one that operates without any direct or apparent effort.

All of these definitions are to say that the city of Jerusalem has the power to sway and influence the opinions of every nation on earth without any direct or apparent effort. You either love or hate Jerusalem. Nations are either for her or against her. Additionally, all nations recognize her dominance as THE holy city.

Chapter 18

1 And after these things I saw another angel come down from heaven, having great power; and the earth was lightened with his glory.

John observes another angel coming down from heaven. This angel had power and glory that lit up the earth.

2 And he cried mightily with a strong voice, saying, Babylon the great is fallen, is fallen, and is become the habitation of devils, and the hold of every foul spirit, and a cage of every unclean and hateful bird.

This angel cried loudly in a strong voice that Babylon had fallen. We have already established that Jerusalem, due to her idolatry, was like Babylon. There are demonic spirits that live there. Jeremiah Chapter 5 verses 24-27 references the cage of unclean and hateful birds by stating,

Neither say they in their heart, Let us now fear the LORD our God, that giveth rain, both the former and the latter, in his season: he reserveth unto us the appointed weeks of the harvest.
Your iniquities have turned away these *things*, and your sins have withholden good *things* from you.
For among my people are found wicked *men*: they lay wait, as he that setteth snares; they set a trap, they catch men.

As a cage is full of birds, so *are* their houses full of deceit: therefore they are become great, and waxen rich.

These are churches with many members, but they are full of deception, and through that deception, the church leaders are very rich. God is talking to Jerusalem, telling them some places of worship are being led by demonic leaders. In my opinion, today, there are demonic church leaders found all over the world.

3 For all nations have drunk of the wine of the wrath of her fornication, and the kings of the earth have committed fornication with her, and the merchants of the earth are waxed rich through the abundance of her delicacies.

Non-believers have turned away from God for their love of money (idol worship). The world has become very materialistic. Commercialism is out of control in many parts of the world. Applying this mentality to Jerusalem, when the third temple is built, the cost of materials for construction will be astronomical. Upon completion, this lavish spending will continue down the same path.

4 And I heard another voice from heaven, saying, Come out of her, my people, that ye be not partakers of her sins, and that ye receive not of her plagues.

John observed another voice from heaven. This voice states a warning to believers to not be like the world. We are to be careful and do not love money more than God so that we do not incur the wrath of God.

5 For her sins have reached unto heaven, and God hath remembered her iniquities.

This city has committed such atrocities against God that He remembers how bad the original Babylon was (hence the naming this city "Babylon") and how there is no difference.

6 Reward her even as she rewarded you, and double unto her double according to her works: in the cup which she hath filled fill to her double.

What this city has given to God, for all of her evil deeds, she will receive double. Fill her cup with double portions of what she has poured out for herself.

7 How much she hath glorified herself, and lived deliciously, so much torment and sorrow give her: for she saith in her heart, I sit a queen, and am no widow, and shall see no sorrow.

This city has glorified herself and lived a life of grandeur. Now she will receive torment and sorrow. This city thinks of itself as a queen, a married queen. Jerusalem was once in covenant with God and was married to Him. She still thinks this is true and that she will be protected.

8 Therefore shall her plagues come in one day, death, and mourning, and famine; and she shall be utterly burned with fire: for strong *is* the Lord God who judgeth her.

The plagues of this city shall come suddenly upon her. This is the abomination of desolation.

9 And the kings of the earth, who have committed fornication and lived deliciously with her, shall bewail her, and lament for her, when they shall see the smoke of her burning.

All the nations who committed idolatry (love of money) with this city, will see her burning and cry out loud at her destruction.

10 Standing afar off for the fear of her torment, saying, Alas, alas, that great city Babylon, that mighty city! for in one hour is thy judgment come.

The nations will watch from a distance her destruction. They will say that great city "Babylon," her destruction has come upon her so suddenly!

11 And the merchants of the earth shall weep and mourn over her; for no man buyeth their merchandise any more:

The merchants do not mourn for the city, but for the money they will lose because she isn't around to buy their stuff.

12 The merchandise of gold, and silver, and precious stones, and of pearls, and fine linen, and purple, and silk, and scarlet, and all thyine wood, and all manner vessels of ivory, and all manner vessels of most precious wood, and of brass, and iron, and marble,

The city (the woman) is wearing similar items as the harlot riding the beast in the last chapter, verse 4. Additionally, these are the same items used either in the construction of the temple or during worship as we shall see shortly.

This is why I believe the city is Jerusalem. Yes, I agree it sounds like America, but the construction of the third temple as well as the day to day operation will require major consumption of these materials.

13 And cinnamon, and odours, and ointments, and frankincense, and wine, and oil, and fine flour, and wheat, and beasts, and sheep, and horses, and chariots, and slaves, and souls of men.

This completes the list of items. This list is practically identical to the one found in the book of Exodus Chapter 25. God is talking to Moses about the required materials needed to build the tabernacle. The best translation is from the New International bible (NIV) stating,

The Lord said to Moses, [2] "Tell the Israelites to bring me an offering. You are to receive the offering for me from everyone whose heart prompts them to give. **³** These are the offerings you are to receive from them: gold, silver and bronze; **⁴** blue, purple and scarlet yarn and fine linen; goat hair; **⁵** ram skins dyed red and another type of durable leather[a]; acacia wood; **⁶** olive oil for the light; spices for the anointing oil and for the fragrant incense; **⁷** and onyx stones and other gems to be mounted on the ephod and breast piece."

At this point, the best way to demonstrate the use of materials for the temple is to let you read them for yourself. These verses (minus the verses about the atonement money) are from Exodus Chapters 25-31 (NIV). The NIV version was used because of its modern day language thereby lessening confusion.

The Ark

¹⁰ "Have them make an ark[b] of acacia wood—two and a half cubits long, a cubit and a half wide, and a cubit and a half high.[c] **¹¹** Overlay it with pure gold, both inside and out, and make a gold molding around it. **¹²** Cast four gold rings for it and fasten them to its four feet, with two rings on one side and two rings on the other. **¹³** Then make poles of acacia wood and overlay them with gold. **¹⁴** Insert the poles into the rings on the sides of the ark to carry it. **¹⁵** The poles are to remain in the rings of this ark; they are not to be removed. **¹⁶** Then put in the ark the tablets of the covenant law, which I will give you."

¹⁷ "Make an atonement cover of pure gold—two and a half cubits long and a cubit and a half wide. **¹⁸** And make two cherubim out of hammered gold at the ends of the cover. **¹⁹** Make one cherub on one end and the second cherub on the other; make the cherubim of one piece with the cover, at the two ends. **²⁰** The cherubim are to have their wings spread upward, overshadowing the cover with them. The cherubim are to face each other, looking toward the cover. **²¹** Place the cover on top of the ark and put in the ark the tablets of the covenant law that I will give you. **²²** There, above the cover between the two cherubim that are over the ark of the covenant law, I will meet with you and give you all my commands for the Israelites."

The Table

²³ "Make a table of acacia wood—two cubits long, a cubit wide and a cubit and a half high.[d]²⁴ Overlay it with pure gold and make a gold molding around it. ²⁵ Also make around it a rim a handbreadth[e] wide and put a gold molding on the rim. ²⁶ Make four gold rings for the table and fasten them to the four corners, where the four legs are. ²⁷ The rings are to be close to the rim to hold the poles used in carrying the table. ²⁸ Make the poles of acacia wood, overlay them with gold and carry the table with them. ²⁹ And make its plates and dishes of pure gold, as well as its pitchers and bowls for the pouring out of offerings. ³⁰ Put the bread of the Presence on this table to be before me at all times."

The Lamp stand

³¹ "Make a lamp stand of pure gold. Hammer out its base and shaft, and make its flowerlike cups, buds and blossoms of one piece with them.³² Six branches are to extend from the sides of the lamp stand—three on one side and three on the other. ³³ Three cups shaped like almond flowers with buds and blossoms are to be on one branch, three on the next branch, and the same for all six branches extending from the lamp stand. ³⁴ And on the lamp stand there are to be four cups shaped like almond flowers with buds and blossoms. ³⁵ One bud shall be under the first pair of branches extending from the lamp stand, a second bud under the second pair, and a third bud under the third pair—six branches in all. ³⁶ The buds and branches shall all be of one piece with the lamp stand, hammered out of pure gold."

³⁷ "Then make its seven lamps and set them up on it so that they light the space in front of it.³⁸ Its wick trimmers and trays are to be of pure gold. ³⁹ A talent[f] of pure gold is to be used for the lamp stand and all these accessories. ⁴⁰ See that you make them according to the pattern shown you on the mountain."

The Tabernacle

26 "Make the tabernacle with ten curtains of finely twisted linen and blue, purple and scarlet yarn, with cherubim woven into them by a skilled worker. **2** All the curtains are to be the same size—twenty-eight cubits long and four cubits wide.[a] **3** Join five of the curtains together, and do the same with the other five. **4** Make loops of blue material along the edge of the end curtain in one set, and do the same with the end curtain in the other set. **5** Make fifty loops on one curtain and fifty loops on the end curtain of the other set, with the loops opposite each other. **6** Then make fifty gold clasps and use them to fasten the curtains together so that the tabernacle is a unit."

7 "Make curtains of goat hair for the tent over the tabernacle—eleven altogether. **8** All eleven curtains are to be the same size—thirty cubits long and four cubits wide.[b] **9** Join five of the curtains together into one set and the other six into another set. Fold the sixth curtain double at the front of the tent. **10** Make fifty loops along the edge of the end curtain in one set and also along the edge of the end curtain in the other set. **11** Then make fifty bronze clasps and put them in the loops to fasten the tent together as a unit. **12** As for the additional length of the tent curtains, the half curtain that is left over is to hang down at the rear of the tabernacle. **13** The tent curtains will be a cubit[c] longer on both sides; what is left will hang over the sides of the tabernacle so as to cover it. **14** Make for the tent a covering of ram skins dyed red, and over that a covering of the other durable leather.[d]"

15 "Make upright frames of acacia wood for the tabernacle. **16** Each frame is to be ten cubits long and a cubit and a half wide,[e] **17** with two projections set parallel to each other. Make all the frames of the tabernacle in this way. **18** Make twenty frames for the south side of the tabernacle **19** and make forty silver bases to go under them—two bases for each frame, one under each projection. **20** For the other side, the north side of the tabernacle, make twenty frames **21** and forty silver bases—two under each frame. **22** Make six frames for the far end, that is, the west end of the tabernacle, **23** and make two frames for the corners at the far end. ²⁴ At these two corners they must be double from the bottom all the way to the top and fitted into a single ring; both shall be like that. ²⁵ So there will be eight frames and sixteen silver bases—two under each frame."

²⁶ "Also make crossbars of acacia wood: five for the frames on one side of the tabernacle, ²⁷ five for those on the other side, and five for the frames on the west, at the far end of the tabernacle. ²⁸ The center crossbar is to extend from end to end at the middle of the frames.²⁹ Overlay the frames with gold and make gold rings to hold the crossbars. Also overlay the crossbars with gold."

³⁰ "Set up the tabernacle according to the plan shown you on the mountain."

³¹ "Make a curtain of blue, purple and scarlet yarn and finely twisted linen, with cherubim woven into it by a skilled worker. ³² Hang it with gold hooks on four posts of acacia wood overlaid with gold and standing on four silver bases.³³ Hang the curtain from the clasps and place the ark of the covenant law behind the curtain. The curtain will separate the Holy Place from the Most Holy Place. ³⁴ Put the atonement cover on the ark of the covenant law in the Most Holy Place. ³⁵ Place the table outside the curtain on the north side of the tabernacle and put the lamp stand opposite it on the south side."

³⁶ "For the entrance to the tent make a curtain of blue, purple and scarlet yarn and finely twisted linen—the work of an embroiderer. ³⁷ Make gold hooks for this curtain and five posts of acacia wood overlaid with gold. And cast five bronze bases for them."

The Altar of Burnt Offering

27 "Build an altar of acacia wood, three cubits[a] high; it is to be square, five cubits long and five cubits wide.[b] ² Make a horn at each of the four corners, so that the horns and the altar are of one piece, and overlay the altar with bronze.³ Make all its utensils of bronze—its pots to remove the ashes, and its shovels, sprinkling bowls, meat forks and fire pans. **4** Make a grating for it, a bronze network, and make a bronze ring at each of the four corners of the network. **5** Put it under the ledge of the altar so that it is halfway up the altar. **6** Make poles of acacia wood for the altar and overlay them with bronze. **7** The poles are to be inserted into the rings so they will be on two sides of the altar when it is carried. **8** Make the altar hollow, out of boards. It is to be made just as you were shown on the mountain."

The Courtyard

9 "Make a courtyard for the tabernacle. The south side shall be a hundred cubits[c] long and is to have curtains of finely twisted linen, **10** with twenty posts and twenty bronze bases and with silver hooks and bands on the posts. **11** The north side shall also be a hundred cubits long and is to have curtains, with twenty posts and twenty bronze bases and with silver hooks and bands on the posts."

12 "The west end of the courtyard shall be fifty cubits[d] wide and have curtains, with ten posts and ten bases. **13** On the east end, toward the sunrise, the courtyard shall also be fifty cubits wide. **14** Curtains fifteen cubits[e] long are to be on one side of the entrance, with three posts and three bases, **15** and curtains fifteen cubits long are to be on the other side, with three posts and three bases."

16 "For the entrance to the courtyard, provide a curtain twenty cubits[f] long, of blue, purple and scarlet yarn and finely twisted linen—the work of an embroiderer—with four posts and four bases. **17** All the posts around the courtyard are to have silver bands and hooks, and bronze bases. **18** The courtyard shall be a hundred cubits long and fifty cubits wide,[g] with curtains of finely twisted linen five cubits[h] high, and with bronze bases. **19** All the other articles used in the service of the tabernacle, whatever their function, including all the tent pegs for it and those for the courtyard, are to be of bronze."

Oil for the Lamp stand

[20] "Command the Israelites to bring you clear oil of pressed olives for the light so that the lamps may be kept burning. [21] In the tent of meeting outside the curtain that shields the ark of the covenant law, Aaron and his sons are to keep the lamps burning before the Lord from evening till morning. This is to be a lasting ordinance among the Israelites for the generations to come."

The Priestly Garments

28 "Have Aaron your brother brought to you from among the Israelites, along with his sons Nadab and Abihu, Eleazar and Ithamar, so they may serve me as priests. [2] Make sacred garments for your brother Aaron to give him dignity and honor. [3] Tell all the skilled workers to whom I have given wisdom in such matters that they are to make garments for Aaron, for his consecration, so he may serve me as priest. [4] These are the garments they are to make: a breast piece, an ephod, a robe, a woven tunic, a turban and a sash. They are to make these sacred garments for your brother Aaron and his sons, so they may serve me as priests. [5] Have them use gold, and blue, purple and scarlet yarn, and fine linen."

The Ephod

[6] "Make the ephod of gold, and of blue, purple and scarlet yarn, and of finely twisted linen—the work of skilled hands. [7] It is to have two shoulder pieces attached to two of its corners, so it can be fastened. [8] Its skillfully woven waistband is to be like it—of one piece with the ephod and made with gold, and with blue, purple and scarlet yarn, and with finely twisted linen."

[9] "Take two onyx stones and engrave on them the names of the sons of Israel [10] in the order of their birth—six names on one stone and the remaining six on the other. [11] Engrave the names of the sons of Israel on the two stones the way a gem cutter engraves a seal. Then mount the stones in gold filigree

settings ¹² and fasten them on the shoulder pieces of the ephod as memorial stones for the sons of Israel. Aaron is to bear the names on his shoulders as a memorial before the Lord. ¹³ Make gold filigree settings ¹⁴ and two braided chains of pure gold, like a rope, and attach the chains to the settings."

The Breast piece

¹⁵ "Fashion a breast piece for making decisions—the work of skilled hands. Make it like the ephod: of gold, and of blue, purple and scarlet yarn, and of finely twisted linen. ¹⁶ It is to be square—a span[a] long and a span wide—and folded double.¹⁷ Then mount four rows of precious stones on it. The first row shall be carnelian, chrysolite and beryl; ¹⁸ the second row shall be turquoise, lapis lazuli and emerald; ¹⁹ the third row shall be jacinth, agate and amethyst; ²⁰ the fourth row shall be topaz, onyx and jasper.[b] Mount them in gold filigree settings. ²¹ There are to be twelve stones, one for each of the names of the sons of Israel, each engraved like a seal with the name of one of the twelve tribes."

²² "For the breast piece make braided chains of pure gold, like a rope. ²³ Make two gold rings for it and fasten them to two corners of the breast piece. ²⁴ Fasten the two gold chains to the rings at the corners of the breast piece, ²⁵ and the other ends of the chains to the two settings, attaching them to the shoulder pieces of the ephod at the front. ²⁶ Make two gold rings and attach them to the other two corners of the breast piece on the inside edge next to the ephod. ²⁷ Make two more gold rings and attach them to the bottom of the shoulder pieces on the front of the ephod, close to the seam just above the waistband of the ephod. ²⁸ The rings of the breast piece are to be tied to the rings of the ephod with blue cord, connecting it to the waistband, so that the breast piece will not swing out from the ephod."

²⁹ "Whenever Aaron enters the Holy Place, he will bear the names of the sons of Israel over his heart on the breast piece of decision as a continuing memorial before the Lord. ³⁰ Also put the Urim and the Thummim in the breast piece,

so they may be over Aaron's heart whenever he enters the presence of the Lord. Thus Aaron will always bear the means of making decisions for the Israelites over his heart before the Lord."

Other Priestly Garments

31 "Make the robe of the ephod entirely of blue cloth, **32** with an opening for the head in its center. There shall be a woven edge like a collar[c] around this opening, so that it will not tear.**33** Make pomegranates of blue, purple and scarlet yarn around the hem of the robe, with gold bells between them. **34** The gold bells and the pomegranates are to alternate around the hem of the robe. **35** Aaron must wear it when he ministers. The sound of the bells will be heard when he enters the Holy Place before the Lord and when he comes out, so that he will not die."

36 "Make a plate of pure gold and engrave on it as on a seal: holy to the Lord. **37** Fasten a blue cord to it to attach it to the turban; it is to be on the front of the turban. **38** It will be on Aaron's forehead, and he will bear the guilt involved in the sacred gifts the Israelites consecrate, whatever their gifts may be. It will be on Aaron's forehead continually so that they will be acceptable to the Lord."

39 "Weave the tunic of fine linen and make the turban of fine linen. The sash is to be the work of an embroiderer. **40** Make tunics, sashes and caps for Aaron's sons to give them dignity and honor.**41** After you put these clothes on your brother Aaron and his sons, anoint and ordain them. Consecrate them so they may serve me as priests."

42 "Make linen undergarments as a covering for the body, reaching from the waist to the thigh.**43** Aaron and his sons must wear them whenever they enter the tent of meeting or approach the altar to minister in the Holy Place, so that they will not incur guilt and die."

"This is to be a lasting ordinance for Aaron and his descendants."

Consecration of the Priests

29 "This is what you are to do to consecrate them, so they may serve me as priests: Take a young bull and two rams without defect. **2** And from the finest wheat flour make round loaves without yeast, thick loaves without yeast and with olive oil mixed in, and thin loaves without yeast and brushed with olive oil. **3** Put them in a basket and present them along with the bull and the two rams. **4** Then bring Aaron and his sons to the entrance to the tent of meeting and wash them with water. **5** Take the garments and dress Aaron with the tunic, the robe of the ephod, the ephod itself and the breast piece. Fasten the ephod on him by its skillfully woven waistband. **6** Put the turban on his head and attach the sacred emblem to the turban. **7** Take the anointing oil and anoint him by pouring it on his head. **8** Bring his sons and dress them in tunics **9** and fasten caps on them. Then tie sashes on Aaron and his sons.[a] The priesthood is theirs by a lasting ordinance."

"Then you shall ordain Aaron and his sons."

10 "Bring the bull to the front of the tent of meeting, and Aaron and his sons shall lay their hands on its head. **11** Slaughter it in the Lord's presence at the entrance to the tent of meeting. **12** Take some of the bull's blood and put it on the horns of the altar with your finger, and pour out the rest of it at the base of the altar. **13** Then take all the fat on the internal organs, the long lobe of the liver, and both kidneys with the fat on them, and burn them on the altar. **14** But burn the bull's flesh and its hide and its intestines outside the camp. It is a sin offering.[b]"

15 "Take one of the rams, and Aaron and his sons shall lay their hands on its head. **16** Slaughter it and take the blood and splash it against the sides of the altar. **17** Cut the ram into pieces and wash the internal organs and the legs, putting them with the head and the other pieces. **18** Then burn the entire ram on the altar. It is a burnt offering to the Lord, a pleasing aroma, a food offering presented to the Lord."

¹⁹ "Take the other ram, and Aaron and his sons shall lay their hands on its head. ²⁰ Slaughter it, take some of its blood and put it on the lobes of the right ears of Aaron and his sons, on the thumbs of their right hands, and on the big toes of their right feet. Then splash blood against the sides of the altar. ²¹ And take some blood from the altar and some of the anointing oil and sprinkle it on Aaron and his garments and on his sons and their garments. Then he and his sons and their garments will be consecrated."

²² "Take from this ram the fat, the fat tail, the fat on the internal organs, the long lobe of the liver, both kidneys with the fat on them, and the right thigh. (This is the ram for the ordination.) ²³ From the basket of bread made without yeast, which is before the Lord, take one round loaf, one thick loaf with olive oil mixed in, and one thin loaf.²⁴ Put all these in the hands of Aaron and his sons and have them wave them before the Lord as a wave offering. ²⁵ Then take them from their hands and burn them on the altar along with the burnt offering for a pleasing aroma to the Lord, a food offering presented to the Lord. ²⁶ After you take the breast of the ram for Aaron's ordination, wave it before the Lord as a wave offering, and it will be your share."

²⁷ "Consecrate those parts of the ordination ram that belong to Aaron and his sons: the breast that was waved and the thigh that was presented.²⁸ This is always to be the perpetual share from the Israelites for Aaron and his sons. It is the contribution the Israelites are to make to the Lord from their fellowship offerings."

²⁹ "Aaron's sacred garments will belong to his descendants so that they can be anointed and ordained in them. ³⁰ The son who succeeds him as priest and comes to the tent of meeting to minister in the Holy Place is to wear them seven days."

³¹ "Take the ram for the ordination and cook the meat in a sacred place. ³² At the entrance to the tent of meeting, Aaron and his sons are to eat the meat of the ram and the bread that is in the basket. ³³ They are to eat these offerings by which atonement was made for their ordination and consecration. But no

one else may eat them, because they are sacred. **34** And if any of the meat of the ordination ram or any bread is left over till morning, burn it up. It must not be eaten, because it is sacred."

35 "Do for Aaron and his sons everything I have commanded you, taking seven days to ordain them. **36** Sacrifice a bull each day as a sin offering to make atonement. Purify the altar by making atonement for it, and anoint it to consecrate it.**37** For seven days make atonement for the altar and consecrate it. Then the altar will be most holy, and whatever touches it will be holy."

38 "This is what you are to offer on the altar regularly each day: two lambs a year old. **39** Offer one in the morning and the other at twilight.**40** With the first lamb offer a tenth of an ephah[c] of the finest flour mixed with a quarter of a hin[d] of oil from pressed olives, and a quarter of a hin of wine as a drink offering. **41** Sacrifice the other lamb at twilight with the same grain offering and its drink offering as in the morning—a pleasing aroma, a food offering presented to the Lord."

42 "For the generations to come this burnt offering is to be made regularly at the entrance to the tent of meeting, before the Lord. There I will meet you and speak to you; **43** there also I will meet with the Israelites, and the place will be consecrated by my glory."

44 "So I will consecrate the tent of meeting and the altar and will consecrate Aaron and his sons to serve me as priests. **45** Then I will dwell among the Israelites and be their God. **46** They will know that I am the Lord their God, who brought them out of Egypt so that I might dwell among them. I am the Lord their God."

The Altar of Incense

30 "Make an altar of acacia wood for burning incense. **2** It is to be square, a cubit long and a cubit wide, and two cubits high[a]—its horns of one piece with it. **3** Overlay the top and all the sides and the horns with pure gold, and make a gold molding around it. ⁴ Make two gold rings for the altar below the molding—two on each of the opposite sides—to hold the poles used to carry it. ⁵ Make the poles of acacia wood and overlay them with gold. ⁶ Put the altar in front of the curtain that shields the ark of the covenant law—before the atonement cover that is over the tablets of the covenant law—where I will meet with you."

⁷ "Aaron must burn fragrant incense on the altar every morning when he tends the lamps. ⁸ He must burn incense again when he lights the lamps at twilight so incense will burn regularly before the Lord for the generations to come. ⁹ Do not offer on this altar any other incense or any burnt offering or grain offering, and do not pour a drink offering on it. ¹⁰ Once a year Aaron shall make atonement on its horns. This annual atonement must be made with the blood of the atoning sin offering[b] for the generations to come. It is most holy to the Lord."

Basin for Washing

¹⁷ Then the Lord said to Moses, ¹⁸ "Make a bronze basin, with its bronze stand, for washing. Place it between the tent of meeting and the altar, and put water in it. ¹⁹ Aaron and his sons are to wash their hands and feet with water from it. ²⁰ Whenever they enter the tent of meeting, they shall wash with water so that they will not die. Also, when they approach the altar to minister by presenting a food offering to the Lord, ²¹ they shall wash their hands and feet so that they will not die. This is to be a lasting ordinance for Aaron and his descendants for the generations to come."

Anointing Oil

²² Then the Lord said to Moses, ²³ "Take the following fine spices: 500 shekels[d] of liquid myrrh, half as much (that is, 250 shekels) of fragrant cinnamon, 250 shekels[e] of fragrant calamus, ²⁴ 500 shekels of cassia—all according to the sanctuary shekel—and a hin[f] of olive oil. ²⁵ Make these into

a sacred anointing oil, a fragrant blend, the work of a perfumer. It will be the sacred anointing oil. **26** Then use it to anoint the tent of meeting, the ark of the covenant law,**27** the table and all its articles, the lamp stand and its accessories, the altar of incense, **28** the altar of burnt offering and all its utensils, and the basin with its stand. **29** You shall consecrate them so they will be most holy, and whatever touches them will be holy."

30 "Anoint Aaron and his sons and consecrate them so they may serve me as priests. **31** Say to the Israelites, 'This is to be my sacred anointing oil for the generations to come. **32** Do not pour it on anyone else's body and do not make any other oil using the same formula. It is sacred, and you are to consider it sacred. **33** Whoever makes perfume like it and puts it on anyone other than a priest must be cut off from their people.'"

Incense

34 Then the Lord said to Moses, "Take fragrant spices—gum resin, onycha and galbanum—and pure frankincense, all in equal amounts, **35** and make a fragrant blend of incense, the work of a perfumer. It is to be salted and pure and sacred.**36** Grind some of it to powder and place it in front of the ark of the covenant law in the tent of meeting, where I will meet with you. It shall be most holy to you. **37** Do not make any incense with this formula for yourselves; consider it holy to the Lord. **38** Whoever makes incense like it to enjoy its fragrance must be cut off from their people."

Bezalel and Oholiab

31 Then the Lord said to Moses, **2** "See, I have chosen Bezalel son of Uri, the son of Hur, of the tribe of Judah, **3** and I have filled him with the Spirit of God, with wisdom, with understanding, with knowledge and with all kinds of skills— **4** to make artistic designs for work in gold, silver and bronze, **5** to cut and set stones, to work in wood, and to engage in all kinds of crafts. **6** Moreover, I have appointed Oholiab son of Ahisamak, of the tribe of Dan, to help him. Also I have given ability to all the skilled workers to make everything I have commanded you: ⁷ the tent of meeting, the ark of the covenant law with the atonement cover on it, and all the other furnishings of the tent— ⁸ the table and its articles, the pure gold lamp stand and all its accessories, the altar of incense, ⁹ the altar of burnt offering and all its utensils, the basin with its stand— ¹⁰ and also the woven garments, both the sacred garments for Aaron the priest and the garments for his sons when they serve as priests, ¹¹ and the anointing oil and fragrant incense for the Holy Place. They are to make them just as I commanded you."

These passages show the use of the items listed in revelation verses 12-13. The only exceptions are thyine wood, upon research, has historically been used to create the special incense needed for temple worship. Marble (although I have read daily temple worship articles and marble is used upon the altar). Slaves, which I'm sure that will be worked in somehow during the construction. That's cheap free labor! And souls of men, which I'm sure that many men will sell their souls to bring the third temple to fruition. Lastly, let's examine the price of the first temple just based on TWO items. The gold and silver. It's is said that the amount of gold used weighed 100,000 talents (about 3,750 tons). Value today: $45 billion. The amount of silver used was 1,000,000 talents (about 37,500 tons). Value today: 10.8 billion. These two items total $55.8 BILLION dollars! This is why the merchants would be wailing!

Back to revelation.

14 And the fruits that thy soul lusted after are departed from thee, and all things which were dainty and goodly are departed from thee, and thou shalt find them no more at all.

Jesus spoke to Jerusalem regarding fruit of the soul. Matthew Chapter 21 verse 43 states,

Therefore say I unto you, The kingdom of God shall be taken from you, and given to a nation bringing forth the fruits thereof.

Jesus told them that He was taking salvation from the "Jews" and was giving it to the Gentiles, and they would produce "fruits." In other words, spread the gospel and create believers throughout the world. Jerusalem will be seeking the kingdom of God but it will not exist anymore. Neither will other things associated with Jesus and righteousness.

Additionally, the line "the fruits that thy soul lusted after," can be the fruit of the spirit mentioned in Galatians Chapter 5 verse 22 stating,

But the fruit of the Spirit is love, joy, peace, long suffering, gentleness, goodness, faith.

These fruits mesh with the next line of things dainty and goodly. Our soul desire these things but usually our free will and humanity prevent us from obtaining these fruits. Nonetheless, these things will not be found in Jerusalem anymore.

15 The merchants of these things, which were made rich by her, shall stand afar off for the fear of her torment, weeping and wailing,

This is a repeat of verses 9 and 10.

16 And saying, Alas, alas, that great city, that was clothed in fine linen, and purple, and scarlet, and decked with gold, and precious stones, and pearls!

Note how this verse mentions that great city. The words "great city" are used specifically in Revelation Chapter 11 verse 8 stating,

And their dead bodies *shall lie* in the street of the great city, which spiritually is called Sodom and Egypt, where also our Lord was crucified.

This city is Jerusalem.

17 For in one hour so great riches is come to nought. And every shipmaster, and all the company in ships, and sailors, and as many as trade by sea, stood afar off,

Suddenly all of the riches (items in the temple) have become useless. All the nations who provided those riches are still observing her destruction from a distance.

18 And cried when they saw the smoke of her burning, saying, What *city is* like unto this great city!

The merchants, still crying over the loss of their money, state there is no city with the extravagance need for the materials used in the temple and during temple sacrifices.

19 And they cast dust on their heads, and cried, weeping and wailing, saying, Alas, alas, that great city, wherein were made rich all that had ships in the sea by reason of her costliness! for in one hour is she made desolate.

The merchants continue to cry profusely over their losses. No more importing those expensive materials. The city has become desolate.

20 Rejoice over her, *thou* heaven, and *ye holy* apostles and prophets; for God hath avenged you on her.

Where have most apostles and prophets come from? Jerusalem. Remember Jezebel, who killed those who worshipped the true God. Remember Saul (who later became Paul) whose mission it was to kill apostles? And countless other apostles and prophets killed in Jerusalem.

21 And a mighty angel took up a stone like a great millstone, and cast *it* into the sea, saying, Thus with violence shall that great city Babylon be thrown down, and shall be found no more at all.

An angel picked up a stone and cast it into the sea destroying that great city "Babylon." This is the utter destruction of idolatrous (fornicating) Babylonian Jerusalem. This Jerusalem has been defiled and is no longer eligible as the bride of Christ. There will be a new Jerusalem, the new bride, as mentioned in Revelation Chapter 21 verses 9-10 stating,

And there came unto me one of the seven angels which had the seven vials full of the seven last plagues, and talked with me, saying, Come hither, I will shew thee the bride, the Lamb's wife.

And he carried me away in the spirit to a great and high mountain, and shewed me that great city, the holy Jerusalem, descending out of heaven from God.

Note the use of the term "great city" applying it to the NEW Jerusalem.

22 And the voice of harpers, and musicians, and of pipers, and trumpeters, shall be heard no more at all in thee; and no craftsman, of whatsoever craft *he be*, shall be found any more in thee; and the sound of a millstone shall be heard no more at all in thee;

The temple has the daily song of the Levitical choir. There were different songs for every day of the week as well as for special holidays. There were instruments. The songs were performed in the morning and in the evening during libations. A libation is defined as: a drink poured out as an offering to a deity. After the atoning sacrifice of Jesus, temple worship is pagan and idolatrous.

The verse goes on to say no workmanship of any kind shall be found. Those who crafted items for the temple were gone.

23 And the light of a candle shall shine no more at all in thee; and the voice of the bridegroom and of the bride shall be heard no more at all in thee: for thy merchants were the great men of the earth; for by thy sorceries were all nations deceived.

This is basically the same thing God said to Jerusalem when He caused them to be conquered by Nebuchadnezzar and became slaves. Jeremiah Chapter 25 verses 9-11 states,

Behold, I will send and take all the families of the north, saith the LORD, and Nebuchadnezzar the king of Babylon, my servant, and will bring them against this land, and against the inhabitants thereof, and against all these nations round about, and will utterly destroy them, and make them an astonishment, and an hissing, and perpetual desolations.

Moreover I will take from them the voice of mirth, and the voice of gladness, the voice of the bridegroom, and the voice of the bride, the sound of the millstones, and the light of the candle.

And this whole land shall be a desolation, *and* an astonishment; and these nations shall serve the king of Babylon seventy years.

Doesn't that almost read exactly like verse 23 of revelation? In both verses, God is saying there will be no signs of Jesus in the city. God did it once (actually several times). He will do it again in the future.

In verse 23, the merchants were the wealthy from all over the earth. All nations were deceived by the sorcery of the city. The Bible describes sorcery as a Hebrew word, awn-nawn which means *to cover*, or *to cloud over*, as in *to behave in a hidden manner* or *occult*, from which the word *cult* originated. Ever heard of Kabbalah? Jewish mysticism? It's hidden and occult, in other words, sorcery.

24 And in her was found the blood of prophets, and of saints, and of all that were slain upon the earth.

This verse reiterates that in this city, there is the blood of the prophets, the saints and through the crucifixion of Jesus, metaphorically, everyone who has ever died since He represents all of mankind.

Chapter 19

1 And after these things I heard a great voice of much people in heaven, saying, Alleluia; Salvation, and glory, and honour, and power, unto the Lord our God:

John heard many voices from heaven giving praise to God.

2 For true and righteous *are* his judgments: for he hath judged the great whore, which did corrupt the earth with her fornication, and hath avenged the blood of his servants at her hand.

The multitude said His judgments are righteous. He had judged and poured out His wrath upon the great whore. Her wickedness and idolatry corrupted the earth and God punished her for killing His servants.

3 And again they said, Alleluia. And her smoke rose up for ever and ever.

The multitude repeated praising God for His vengeance. The smoke of the great whore burned and rose up forever and ever. That is some fire, eternal smoke. Wow.

4 And the four and twenty elders and the four beasts fell down and worshipped God that sat on the throne, saying, Amen; Alleluia.

The twenty four elders and the four beasts fell down before the throne, before God saying amen and alleluia. For He is worthy to be praised.

5 And a voice came out of the throne, saying, Praise our God, all ye his servants, and ye that fear him, both small and great.

John heard a voice coming from the throne saying praise God, all servants and all that fear Him, small and great, everyone.

6 And I heard as it were the voice of a great multitude, and as the voice of many waters, and as the voice of mighty thunderings, saying, Alleluia: for the Lord God omnipotent reigneth.

John heard the voices of the multitude. It sounded like many waters and thunder. They said alleluia for God is omnipotent and He reigns.

7 Let us be glad and rejoice, and give honour to him: for the marriage of the Lamb is come, and his wife hath made herself ready.

It's time to be happy! And honor God! For the Lamb (Jesus) is about to get married and His wife is ready. Now that the old Jerusalem is destroyed. New Jerusalem is ready! Hallelujah!

8 And to her was granted that she should be arrayed in fine linen, clean and white: for the fine linen is the righteousness of saints.

She is wearing clean, white fine linen. The clothing of believers.

9 And he saith unto me, Write, Blessed *are* they which are called unto the marriage supper of the Lamb. And he saith unto me, These are the true sayings of God.

John was told to write and tell mankind that believers are blessed to be attending the marriage of Jesus. He told John this is the truth from God.

10 And I fell at his feet to worship him. And he said unto me, See *thou do it* not: I am thy fellow servant, and of thy brethren that have the testimony of Jesus: worship God: for the testimony of Jesus is the spirit of prophecy.

John fell at His feet and worshipped Him. The person John had been conversing with was a fellow follower (believer) and servant of Christ. He told John not to worship him. He stated, "worship only God because only God is worthy to be praised." As I write this book, I had this exact thought earlier today. I am not special. I am merely a messenger, an instrument, like a pen, that God has chosen to use for His message.

11 And I saw heaven opened, and behold a white horse; and he that sat upon him *was* called Faithful and True, and in righteousness he doth judge and make war.

John saw heaven open. There was a white horse and upon that horse sat Jesus. He is called Faithful. We can always rely on Jesus. His ways are not our ways; His thoughts are not our thoughts. He is called True. Jesus is not man that He should lie. We can rely on Jesus for everything. Thank you God! Jesus, using His supreme righteousness goes into the battle of Armageddon.

12 His eyes *were* as a flame of fire, and on his head *were* many crowns; and he had a name written, that no man knew, but he himself.

Jesus has eyes like flaming fire. He has many crowns upon His head. This symbolism tells us that He is the king of kings and Lord of Lords. There is no ruler equal to Him. He has a secret name that only He knows written upon Him.

13 And he *was* clothed with a vesture dipped in blood: and his name is called The Word of God.

The clothing that Jesus is wearing will become stained with the blood of His enemies during the battle. He is the Word of God.

14 And the armies *which were* in heaven followed him upon white horses, clothed in fine linen, white and clean.

These are the believers who have been reaped (taken) from the earth years before this return to earth. We will be the army, with Jesus as our leader during the battle of Armageddon. We are wearing clothing made of fine linen made white and clean by the blood of the Lamb. Being a believer in Jesus has made us immortal. We are no longer "human." We have become spiritual beings.

15 And out of his mouth goeth a sharp sword, that with it he should smite the nations: and he shall rule them with a rod of iron: and he treadeth the winepress of the fierceness and wrath of Almighty God.

The fact that this sharp sword proceeds out of His mouth emphasizes that He is the word. His words are so powerful that He can slay evil just by speaking. Think of it as in the book of Genesis, where God created everything just by speaking. This will be the opposite. Jesus will rule with a rod of iron. This means it will be a very different world from the one in which we are living now. This seems harsh, but remember, like the parable of the landowner, He owns the land, He makes the rules, He can do what He wants with His stuff. Secondly, consider the alternative. Hell. No thanks.

As for Jesus treading the wine press, in Isaiah Chapter 63 verses 2-6 (NET version states it the best)

Why do you look like someone who has stomped on grapes in a vat?
I have stomped grapes in the winepress all by myself;
no one from the nations joined me.
I stomped on them in my anger;
I trampled them down in my rage.
Their juice splashed on my garments,
and stained all my clothes.

For I looked forward to the day of vengeance,
and then payback time arrived.

Love the metaphors.

16 And he hath on *his* vesture and on his thigh a name written, KING OF KINGS, AND LORD OF LORDS.

John observes Jesus wearing His clothing and upon His thigh was written King of Kings and Lord of Lords. Remember this was represented by His multiple crowns upon His head as well. The multiple display of symbolism leads me to think He is saying, "I am in charge now and don't you forget it!"

17 And I saw an angel standing in the sun; and he cried with a loud voice, saying to all the fowls that fly in the midst of heaven, Come and gather yourselves together unto the supper of the great God;

John saw an angel calling out to the birds in a loud voice. He was calling the birds of prey that fly high above the earth in search of dead flesh to consume. They are being called because there will be so much dead flesh after the battle of Armageddon that it will be as a supper Jesus is giving them.

18 That ye may eat the flesh of kings, and the flesh of captains, and the flesh of mighty men, and the flesh of horses, and of them that sit on them, and the flesh of all *men, both* free and bond, both small and great.

The birds gather and eat the flesh of the dead. There are men from all walks of life who died in this battle. It doesn't matter to God who you are nor what you have, for He is no respecter of persons. This is found in Romans Chapter 2 verses 6-12 stating,

Who will render to every man according to his deeds:
To them who by patient continuance in well doing seek for glory and honour

and immortality, eternal life:
But unto them that are contentious, and do not obey the truth, but obey unrighteousness, indignation and wrath,
Tribulation and anguish, upon every soul of man that doeth evil, of the Jew first, and also of the Gentile;
But glory, honour, and peace, to every man that worketh good, to the Jew first, and also to the Gentile:
For there is no respect of persons with God.

19 And I saw the beast, and the kings of the earth, and their armies, gathered together to make war against him that sat on the horse, and against his army.

This is the last stand of the antichrist. The kings of the earth and their armies are gathered together in Megiddo. They are prepared to fight Jesus and His army of believers. Jesus and His army are comprised of immortals. On the antichrist's side, the only immortal person is him! It's like the old adage, the blind leading the blind!

20 And the beast was taken, and with him the false prophet that wrought miracles before him, with which he deceived them that had received the mark of the beast, and them that worshipped his image. These both were cast alive into a lake of fire burning with brimstone.

The antichrist and the false prophet who performed miracles and deceived the non-believers into following the beast are thrown ALIVE into a lake of fire. The kingdom of the antichrist is finished.

21 And the remnant were slain with the sword of him that sat upon the horse, which *sword* proceeded out of his mouth: and all the fowls were filled with their flesh.

Those left alive were killed by Jesus using the sword from His mouth, which is the word of God. All of the predatory birds called to the supper of God were made full from eating the dead. That is a very graphic depiction. Nearly as horrific as a plague from the wrath of God. This, among many, is another reason I follow Christ. I cannot fathom being on the losing team. This isn't some meager game. Winner takes all (eternal life) and the loser spends ETERNITY in hell, being tormented. I can't do that. Thank you Jesus for dying for me and all of mankind. Your sacrifice was AND is a gift for all human beings to receive and enjoy. Hallelujah to the Lamb of God!!

Chapter 20

1 And I saw an angel come down from heaven, having the key of the bottomless pit and a great chain in his hand.

Remember Revelation Chapter 9 verse 11? The angel with the key to the bottomless pit name in Hebrew is Abaddon (which means destruction in Hebrew) and in Greek, it is Apollyon. This is not the devil.

2 And he laid hold on the dragon, that old serpent, which is the Devil, and Satan, and bound him a thousand years,

The angel grabbed the devil and threw him into the bottomless pit (hell). Note that the devil is in hell, but the antichrist and the false prophet are in the everlasting lake of fire. They are done.

3 And cast him into the bottomless pit, and shut him up, and set a seal upon him, that he should deceive the nations no more, till the thousand years should be fulfilled: and after that he must be loosed a little season.

Satan will be released from hell after Jesus reigns on earth for 1,000 years. He cannot deceive the world during this time. This is confirmation that there is deceit about everything in this current world.

As a mere mortal having mortal thoughts, 1,000 years seem like a long time. The great part about this is, as a believer, we will be immortal! No more death for us! When Jesus caught us up in the air after He came in the clouds (rapture) before the wrath of God, we changed from mortal to immortal in the twinkling of an eye! Amen! No more death!

4 And I saw thrones, and they sat upon them, and judgment was given unto them: and *I saw* the souls of them that were beheaded for the witness of Jesus, and for the word of God, and which had not worshipped the beast, neither his image, neither had received *his* mark upon their foreheads, or in their hands; and they lived and reigned with Christ a thousand years.

John saw many thrones and the beings that sat upon them. They were being judged for their time on earth. John saw those individuals who were beheaded for believing in Jesus and for resisting the antichrist's parlor tricks. Those souls lived and reigned with Jesus for 1,000 years! Although these are saints, we will be judged for what we did with the gospel of Jesus. Things such as, did we spread the gospel during our time as a believer? Did we keep it to ourselves? We will be judged according to our GOOD works. Hence, why I finally gave in to write this book. It was the right thing to do. The gospel, especially eternal life verses eternal damnation is TOO important not to tell anyone!

5 But the rest of the dead lived not again until the thousand years were finished. This *is* the first resurrection.

The other souls that died without believing in Jesus remained dead. They must stay in their graves until the 1,000 years is completed.

6 Blessed and holy *is* he that hath part in the first resurrection: on such the second death hath no power, but they shall be priests of God and of Christ, and shall reign with him a thousand years.

Believers that are alive now and either die before the return of Jesus or those believers that are alive when He returns are a part of this group. We will never die again. We will be priests of God and shall rule with Him forever.

7 And when the thousand years are expired, Satan shall be loosed out of his prison,

After 1,000 years, the devil is released from hell.

8 And shall go out to deceive the nations which are in the four quarters of the earth, Gog and Magog, to gather them together to battle: the number of whom *is* as the sand of the sea.

The mission of the devil is to continue where he left off, deceiving the world. Trying to capture mankind and send them to the everlasting lake of fire with him. That's his next stop when God is completely done with him. What is amazing is that he will gather as many people as he can for another battle against Christ! Wasn't he watching the last battle? Did you not see the outcome? That's just pure wickedness.

9 And they went up on the breadth of the earth, and compassed the camp of the saints about, and the beloved city: and fire came down from God out of heaven, and devoured them.

Satan and His army went across the earth and tried to snare believers who missed the rapture. These individuals most likely were born during the 1,000 year reign of Christ. Remember anyone who did not go with Jesus in the rapture remained mortal. If you became a believer AFTER that, at some point in time you died.

Mortals cannot live 1,000 years. Many, many, generations have lived and died since the wrath of God has been poured out, and during that time, I'm sure there will be believers who will be alive when the devil is released. God rains fire from heaven and it consumes the devil's army. No more devil! No more deceit! Amen!

10 And the devil that deceived them was cast into the lake of fire and brimstone, where the beast and the false prophet *are*, and shall be tormented day and night for ever and ever.

Now the devil can join his "son" the antichrist and his "friend" the false prophet. They will be tormented in the lake of fire FOREVER! Forever is a LONG time and there will be torment? Thank you Jesus for saving me! Hallelujah! Praise the Lamb of God!

11 And I saw a great white throne, and him that sat on it, from whose face the earth and the heaven fled away; and there was found no place for them.

John saw the great white throne of God. Currently, the face of God is so holy and righteous that if we saw it as mortals, we would die instantly. That is incredible. There isn't a place for our current earth or heaven in the sight of God. They will be replaced.

12 And I saw the dead, small and great, stand before God; and the books were opened: and another book was opened, which is *the book* of life: and the dead were judged out of those things which were written in the books, according to their works.

John saw the dead. Whether they were rich or poor, free or slave, they stood before God to be judged for their time on earth. During this judgment, there will be good (believers) who lived during the 1,000 year reign and there will be bad (non-believers) who lived during that time.

13 And the sea gave up the dead which were in it; and death and hell delivered up the dead which were in them: and they were judged every man according to their works.

Every person who has lived since the devil went to hell was in heaven being judged. This included those in the sea (if they died at sea or was buried there).

Souls from hell were there as well. If you die at any point in time and you don't believe in Christ, you are going to hell. There are age limits, if you are wondering about babies and children. You have to be able to accept Jesus Christ as your personal savior. If you are a baby or small child, you cannot make that choice.

That is what being baptized is all about, choosing to believe in Jesus. Moreover, this is why newborns/babies should not be baptized. They have not chosen anything.

14 And death and hell were cast into the lake of fire. This is the second death.

God is going to throw death and hell into the lake of fire. That is a "I am the boss" gesture! God is so powerful that He can destroy death AND hell! I know He created them, but the mere thought of His ability to do it, just blows my mind. God is truly AWESOME! Amen!

15 And whosoever was not found written in the book of life was cast into the lake of fire.

Non-believers will be cast into the everlasting lake of fire. I know there are people in this world who have done truly evil things. I know that these people, especially in the eyes of God, deserve this fate, but as a fellow human being, it hurts me to think there are people who will be tormented forever. They will never be able to have hopes and dreams. Won't be able to love, no matter what they loved, ever again.

These thoughts, that feeling, is another reason for this book. If it saves just one person from that never-ending nightmare of torture and suffering, my mission will be accomplished. Amen.

Chapter 21

1 And I saw a new heaven and a new earth: for the first heaven and the first earth were passed away; and there was no more sea.

John saw a new heaven and a new earth. Remember in the last chapter, the old ones were no longer found? I can imagine that the old earth would have some miles on it! After the wrath of God has been poured out and after all the years of abuse by mankind, yeah, it's time for a new one! Furthermore, I'm sure the same thing could be said of the sea. It is difficult to imagine a world without any water. Just looking at a map, practically the entire world is water. For it to be removed, will be amazing.

2 And I John saw the holy city, new Jerusalem, coming down from God out of heaven, prepared as a bride adorned for her husband.

John observed a brand new city of Jerusalem coming down from heaven looking as beautiful as a bride does on her wedding day.

3 And I heard a great voice out of heaven saying, Behold, the tabernacle of God *is* with men, and he will dwell with them, and they shall be his people, and God himself shall be with them, *and be* their God.

John heard a great voice from heaven proclaiming the people on earth have a new tabernacle (technically, this is the FOURTH temple, but it is not a building). This tabernacle is Jesus Christ. He will be with us and He will love us as a loving parent loves his children. He will be our God. Thank you Jesus.

4 And God shall wipe away all tears from their eyes; and there shall be no more death, neither sorrow, nor crying, neither shall there be any more pain: for the former things are passed away.

God shall wipe away our tears. We will never experience death (it's burning in the lake of fire) sorrow, crying, nor pain anymore. These are all "passed away" from us. Every time I come to this verse, ironically, it makes me want to cry. I have always thought this is one of the most loving, beautiful things to look forward to as a believer in Christ. We have all experienced heartache, and for God to take it away from us, touches my soul. It reminds me of a loving parent who comforts their child when something is wrong. Having the most powerful being in the universe comforting me, us, is worth every moment of pain, sorrow, and every tear shed. Just to receive His love will be great!

5 And he that sat upon the throne said, Behold, I make all things new. And he said unto me, Write: for these words are true and faithful.

John observed Jesus sitting on the throne. He told John, "write these words for they are faithful and true." And I believe they are, Jesus, I believe. Amen.

6 And he said unto me, It is done. I am Alpha and Omega, the beginning and the end. I will give unto him that is athirst of the fountain of the water of life freely.

Jesus said to John that everything is complete. Jesus is the alpha and the omega. The beginning and the end. It started with Him and He finished it. The devil tried to put a wrinkle in His divine plan, but He ironed it all out.

All who are thirsty shall receive the water of life without restraint from this moment on from Him.

7 He that overcometh shall inherit all things; and I will be his God, and he shall be my son.

Jesus states the individual who makes it to this point in time will inherit everything that should have been ours from the beginning of time. God is our father and we are His children. Thanks dad. Thank you for loving me as much as you do.

8 But the fearful, and unbelieving, and the abominable, and murderers, and whoremongers, and sorcerers, and idolaters, and all liars, shall have their part in the lake which burneth with fire and brimstone: which is the second death.

Unfortunately, all non-believing wicked people will be sent to be tormented in the everlasting lake of fire. They will see death for the second time. Once cast into the lake, there will be no parents, no love, no comfort, nothing. Forever.

9 And there came unto me one of the seven angels which had the seven vials full of the seven last plagues, and talked with me, saying, Come hither, I will shew thee the bride, the Lamb's wife.

John was approached by one of the seven angels that held the vials. He wanted to show John who the bride of Christ is, the Lamb's wife.

10 And he carried me away in the spirit to a great and high mountain, and shewed me that great city, the holy Jerusalem, descending out of heaven from God,

The angel took John as a spirit to a high mountain and pointed out that great city (there is that term "great city" again from chapters 17 and 18). The bride is the new, Holy city of Jerusalem coming down from heaven.

11 Having the glory of God: and her light *was* like unto a stone most precious, even like a jasper stone, clear as crystal;

The city was shining as bright as God. The light appeared clear like crystal.

12 And had a wall great and high, *and* had twelve gates, and at the gates twelve angels, and names written thereon, which are *the names* of the twelve tribes of the children of Israel:

There was a Great Wall that had 12 gates. The gates had 12 angels. These gates had the names of the 12 tribes of Israel upon them.

13 On the east three gates; on the north three gates; on the south three gates; and on the west three gates.

In all four directions, there were three gates. This equals 12.

14 And the wall of the city had twelve foundations, and in them the names of the twelve apostles of the Lamb.

The wall of the new city had 12 foundations. These foundations held the names of the 12 apostles of Jesus.

15 And he that talked with me had a golden reed to measure the city, and the gates thereof, and the wall thereof.

John observed the angel who measured the city, the wall, and the gates with a golden reed.

16 And the city lieth foursquare, and the length is as large as the breadth: and he measured the city with the reed, twelve thousand furlongs. The length and the breadth and the height of it are equal.

The city is like a square. It is as long as it is wide. The angel measured the city. It is 12,000 furlongs. That's 1,500 miles in length, width, and height.

17 And he measured the wall thereof, an hundred *and* forty *and* four cubits, *according to* the measure of a man, that is, of the angel.

The angel measured the wall. It was 144 cubits. That is 216 feet in human measurements, especially American.

18 And the building of the wall of it was *of* jasper: and the city *was* pure gold, like unto clear glass.

The building of the wall was jasper. The city was made of pure gold as clear as glass. This sounds like the holy temple in Jerusalem.

19 And the foundations of the wall of the city *were* garnished with all manner of precious stones. The first foundation *was* jasper; the second, sapphire; the third, a chalcedony; the fourth, an emerald;

Here are the precious stones that were in the priest's breastplate required for temple worship. These "stones" are foundations for the wall of the city.

20 The fifth, sardonyx; the sixth, sardius; the seventh, chrysolite; the eighth, beryl; the ninth, a topaz; the tenth, a chrysoprasus; the eleventh, a jacinth; the twelfth, an amethyst.

This verse continues to describe each layer of foundation made from precious stones.

21 And the twelve gates *were* twelve pearls; every several gate was of one pearl: and the street of the city *was* pure gold, as it were transparent glass.

Here are the famously mentioned "heavenly pearly gates". The city streets are made of gold. Sounds beautiful.

22 And I saw no temple therein: for the Lord God Almighty and the Lamb are the temple of it.

There is no temple in this city. God the Father and Jesus Christ comprise the temple.

23 And the city had no need of the sun, neither of the moon, to shine in it: for the glory of God did lighten it, and the Lamb *is* the light thereof.

The city did not need the sun nor the moon. The glory of God the Father shines bright like the sun along with the light of the Lamb. Jesus did say that He is the way, the truth, and the light.

24 And the nations of them which are saved shall walk in the light of it: and the kings of the earth do bring their glory and honour into it.

All believers, no matter what background they are from, shall walk in the light that shines from the city. The new kings of the earth (believers who were raptured are now kings on the new earth. They will rule with Jesus forever.

25 And the gates of it shall not be shut at all by day: for there shall be no night there.

The gates to the city will always be open. There is no more night time. That is hard to imagine. Darkness does not exist anymore. Things will be so very different in this new world.

26 And they shall bring the glory and honour of the nations into it.

Believers will bring glory and honor from every nation, with different backgrounds and nationalities to the city. In my opinion, this is how the current situation with Jerusalem should be on earth.

27 And there shall in no wise enter into it any thing that defileth, neither *whatsoever* worketh abomination, or *maketh* a lie: but they which are written in the Lamb's book of life.

Basically, anything that is wicked, evil, and deceitful shall not enter into the city. Only believers whose name was found in the book of life are allowed inside the gates.

Chapter 22

1 And he shewed me a pure river of water of life, clear as crystal, proceeding out of the throne of God and of the Lamb.

John saw a river. This was the river of life, undefiled, coming from the throne of God the Father and Jesus.

2 In the midst of the street of it, and on either side of the river, *was there* the tree of life, which bare twelve *manner of* fruits, *and* yielded her fruit every month: and the leaves of the tree *were* for the healing of the nations.

John saw that on both sides of the river were trees of life. Not just one like in the Garden of Eden, but TREES, plural! These trees produce 12 different kinds of fruit, one for each month (fruit of the month club, anyone)? The leaves have the ability to heal. How cool would that be to see now? It will be just as cool to see it in paradise.

3 And there shall be no more curse: but the throne of God and of the Lamb shall be in it; and his servants shall serve him:

There are no more curses. God the Father and Jesus are there and so are we, the believers, His servants.

4 And they shall see his face; and his name *shall be* in their foreheads.

We will finally get to see the face of God without dying. This is one item that tops my list regarding heaven. I want to know what God looks like and look Him square in His eyes. God will write His name on our foreheads. This is "the mark" you will want to take, gladly! This is where the antichrist stole his mark of the beast for nonbelievers. The devil is so unoriginal.

5 And there shall be no night there; and they need no candle, neither light of the sun; for the Lord God giveth them light: and they shall reign for ever and ever.

This is restating there will be no night time in paradise. No light needed whatsoever. Jesus Christ will shine so bright, that He will be the only light we will ever need for all eternity. Amen.

6 And he said unto me, These sayings *are* faithful and true: and the Lord God of the holy prophets sent his angel to shew unto his servants the things which must shortly be done.

Jesus told John everything is faithful and true. Jesus sent His angel to show believers the things that must be accomplished soon.

7 *Behold, I come quickly: blessed is he that keepeth the sayings of the prophecy of this book.*

Jesus said He will come quickly. Everyone who keeps (in his or her heart) the prophecy of the book of revelation, will be blessed.
We receive a blessing just for believing every word Jesus spoke in revelation. Thank you! Hallelujah to the Lamb of God!

8 And I John saw these things, and heard *them*. And when I had heard and seen, I fell down to worship before the feet of the angel which shewed me these things.

John saw and heard everything. John was so moved by what he saw and heard that he fell down before the angel to worship him.

9 Then saith he unto me, See *thou do it* not: for I am thy fellow servant, and of thy brethren the prophets, and of them which keep the sayings of this book: worship God.

Previously, John was told not to worship fellow servants nor anyone else. No one is worthy to be worshipped except God.

10 And he saith unto me, Seal not the sayings of the prophecy of this book: for the time is at hand.

The angel told John not to seal up the book of revelation (unlike Daniel who was told to seal up his writings until our time). It is time for the world to understand the events that are coming soon.

11 He that is unjust, let him be unjust still: and he which is filthy, let him be filthy still: and he that is righteous, let him be righteous still: and he that is holy, let him be holy still.

The angel said the individual that is unjust and filthy, let them continue on living that way. The individual that is righteous and holy, let them continue on living that way.

12 *And, behold, I come quickly; and my reward is with me, to give every man according as his work shall be.*

Jesus restates that He will come quickly, and when He does, He has rewards for every believer according to their life as a Christian.

13 *I am Alpha and Omega, the beginning and the end, the first and the last.*

Jesus said He is the alpha and omega. The first AND the last. The one in the beginning and the one in the end.

14 Blessed *are* they that do his commandments, that they may have right to the tree of life, and may enter in through the gates into the city.

Believers are blessed for living their lives like the life of Jesus although we are still just human. That is not an excuse, but a mere statement of fact. We are believers, but we are still made of sinful flesh. For there is none righteous, no not one. We are all sinners. Believers AND non-believers. The only difference is believers have Jesus to help us, guide us, show us, and save us from ourselves. All we have to do is ask for forgiveness (repent).

15 For without *are* dogs, and sorcerers, and whoremongers, and murderers, and idolaters, and whosoever loveth and maketh a lie.

The new city will not have any dogs in it. Sorry dog lovers. Maybe outside of the city? There will be no evil in the city. Now that will be paradise on earth! This is how it should have been for us from the beginning.

16 *I Jesus have sent mine angel to testify unto you these things in the churches. I am the root and the offspring of David, and the bright and morning star.*

Jesus states He has sent His angel to testify to these writings. Jesus is the root and the offspring of David. He is the bright and morning star. Which is why there will always be light in His holy presence. Amen!

17 And the Spirit and the bride say, Come. And let him that heareth say, Come. And let him that is athirst come. And whosoever will, let him take the water of life freely.
The spirit and the bride said come (understand). All that have ears and can understand what is written should accept these words and believe they are

true. If you are seeking the truth (athirst), take the gift of life that Jesus gives to ANYONE who will drink (believe).

18 For I testify unto every man that heareth the words of the prophecy of this book, If any man shall add unto these things, God shall add unto him the plagues that are written in this book:

Anyone who hears the prophecy of revelation and adds anything to it shall be cursed with the plagues that are written His book. This verse was a source of great concern for me as I wrote my book. I prayed about this and the book you are reading is the answer I received. Thank you Jesus!

19 And if any man shall take away from the words of the book of this prophecy, God shall take away his part out of the book of life, and out of the holy city, and *from* the things which are written in this book.

Anyone who takes anything from the words of revelation, God will take that person from the book of life, out of the holy city, and from anything good written in revelation.

20 He which testifieth these things saith, *Surely I come quickly.* Amen. Even so, come, Lord Jesus.

John wrote that Jesus testified to everything that was said in revelation. Jesus adds that He is coming quickly. Amen! John replied, even so, which means despite the wrath and judgment coming with His return, come to us Lord Jesus.

21 The grace of our Lord Jesus Christ *be* with you all. Amen.

This verse sums up another reason why I gave in to God and wrote this book. It means God wants the grace, the blessing of Jesus Christ to be with us all. Every human being alive on earth right now. God wants no flesh to perish, but to obtain everlasting life by accepting Jesus Christ as their savior. Jesus, in the book of John Chapter 5 verse 24 states,

Verily, verily, I say unto you, He that heareth my word, and believeth on him that sent me, hath everlasting life, and shall not come into condemnation; but is passed from death unto life.

I hope and pray that this book helps someone understand that no matter what you have done, no matter who you are, God the father, Jesus, and the Holy Spirit loves you and wants you to live forever with Him. Not to suffer for eternity. Neither do I.

I am very blessed and very grateful to know the truth. To believe in Jesus and on Jesus. I have believed since I was 11 years old.

Eternity is a long time. This isn't a dress rehearsal. This life is the main event. To all who have read, understood and accepted Christ into your heart, and also to all of mankind, there is hope in the Lord Jesus Christ. The grace of our Lord Jesus Christ BE with you all! Amen.

Acknowledgements:

First and foremost, I want to thank God the Father, Jesus Christ and the Holy Spirit for convincing me through discernment (and constant conviction) to write this book. Thank you for guiding me, answering my prayers, and helping me to complete this endeavor.

Thank you to my daughters Ivana and Veronika for your love, understanding and patience through this process. I love you both very much.

Thank you to my late son, Alexander L. Martin. You have inspired me, given me strength I didn't think I had and helped me to soar high enough to touch the stars. I will always love you.

Thank you to my niece, Ieshia L. Million for all of your love and support through this project. You have held me up when I was down and pulled me back from the ledge. Your support has been invaluable to me and I am beyond grateful. I love you.

Thank you to my brother, Larry Million, whose courage and strength in his life inspired me to get through this project. I love you.

Thank you Charles E. Clay, Jr. for everything you have done for me during this process. You gave me the impetus to start this project and a reason to pursue it with everything I had left and that was nothing. I will be forever grateful.

Thank you for your loving friendship and support, Vincent Walls and Selena Tigglers. You keep me grounded, make me laugh when I need it the most, and lend me your ear in times of trouble. I am grateful for all that you have done.

Thank you to everyone who has worked on the creation of this book, the editors, copywriters, graphic artists, and printers. Without your help, this book would not exist.

Thank you Pastor Steven Anderson for your inspiration, explanation and knowledge of the book of revelation. Through God, you changed my life.

To anyone that I am forgetting but has touched my life, I thank you with all of my heart.

Bibliography

All biblical verses are from the KJV bible.

The Holy Bible, King James Version. Cambridge Edition: 1769; *King James Bible Online*, 2017. www.kingjamesbibleonline.org.

Verse in Chapter 2: ISV Bible

Verses from the book of Isaiah Chapter 63: NET Bible

Items needed for the third temple in Chapter 18: NIV Bible. Used with permission. All rights reserved.

www.ingramcontent.com/pod-product-compliance
Lightning Source LLC
Chambersburg PA
CBHW031417290426
44110CB00011B/422